Social Work Assessment

Social Work Assessment

RUBEN MARTIN

Series Editors: Jonathan Parker and Greta Bradley

LearningMatters

First published in 2010 by Learning Matters Ltd

British Library Cataloguing in Publication Data
A CIP record for this book is available from the British Library

ISBN 978 1 84445 293 4

This book is also available in the following ebook formats:
Adobe ebook ISBN: 9781844457076
EPUB ebook: ISBN: 9781844457069
Kindle ISBN: 9781844459940

Text and cover design by Code 5 Design Associates Ltd
Project management by Deer Park Productions, Tavistock
Typeset by PDQ Typesetting Ltd, Newcastle-under-Lyme
Printed and bound in Great Britain by Bell & Bain Ltd, Glasgow

Learning Matters Ltd
33 Southernhay East
Exeter EX1 1NX
Tel: 01392 215560
info@learningmatters.co.uk
www.learningmatters.co.uk

Contents

Dedication

To the memory of Julia Hazel Martin

24 April 1971 – 2 April 2008

Acknowledgements

I am indebted to work colleagues, students, service users and carers for information and ideas that have influenced me, and my writing. I have learnt much from them over the years. Material from personal discussions, handouts, student academic assignments and the experiences of service users and carers, particularly when I have arranged for them to come to talk to students, have found their way into this book. They are therefore contributors to it, although they may not realise it.

During the process of writing, practitioner colleagues agreed to let me 'pick their brains', share work experiences and give me feedback on relevant chapters. I am particularly grateful to Alison Fullarton, Richard Munn, Cath Slater, Brenda Casells and Nick Whiting, and also to Professor David Shemmings. They have enhanced my work and updated me on developments, but any inaccuracies are my responsibility.

I would like to thank Learning Matters commissioning editor Luke Block for his initial help, development editor Kate Lodge for her careful guidance, and series editor Professor Jonathan Parker for his invaluable feedback and suggestions.

Finally, I must express my personal gratitude to my wife Kay for her loving support and encouragement, and for the long-suffering way in which she has allowed me priority over the use of our computer during so many evenings and weekends.

Introduction

If you have got as far as starting to read this introduction, you are presumably interested in assessments that social workers undertake as part of their work. You are likely to be a student on a social work degree programme, or interested for some other related reason. Although aimed primarily at social work students starting their course, this book contains sufficient depth to be a continuing resource afterwards.

Assessing people we come across is a natural human activity and part of interacting with each other. I was recently travelling with three passengers in my car and, while I concentrated mainly on the road, my friends chatted about mutual acquaintances in terms of their usual clothing and what it said about them. A relatively young woman was considered 'frumpy' due to her customary unfashionable and plain clothing. A father of two small children was said to be 'trendy' due to his practice of buying the latest men's fashion or trends. There was some surprise expressed that he regularly bought his own clothes with such successful results, something they thought was not easy for a man to do without female help. My friends were making assessments and judgements. In so doing they had to come to some agreement about what is fashionable or not, for whom and what current trends are, as there can be differences of opinion about these and they can change over the years. My friends' assessments involved *normative values* – a term used for how things should or ought to be, what is good and acceptable or bad and unacceptable. The use of normative values implicit in judgements is something to guard against when our aim is to be professional in our assessments.

This might be further illustrated by my reading of the first entry on a reflective diary written by new social work students in a relatively small communications skills group of 15 to 18 people. I had arranged the chairs in a circle, rather than rows, as I wanted to generate participation and interaction from the beginning. In reading the diary that students are required to keep for assessment, I noted how many said that on the first meeting they wondered what the other students would be like. Some thought they were younger than others there, others older than the majority. Some perceived other students as more confident or as having more experience. Students compared themselves with the rest in terms of age, gender, ethnicity and other characteristics. This continued with a getting-to-know-you initial exercise that involved talking in pairs, which reassured some students. At least by talking to someone they were starting to make an assessment of that person based on given information rather than perceptions, feelings and normative values.

So, you may be tempted to think that social work assessment is relatively simple, dependent on asking a few right questions. However, as soon as we start exploring what is involved we see that there are many issues involved, such as to what standard or judgement are we making an assessment, how objective can any assessment be, how accurate is any information we gather for assessment, and can we, and should we, avoid our perceptions and feelings? Social work takes place in a range of sectors (e.g. statutory, voluntary, private) and in a variety of settings (e.g. community, day care, residential). Social work is offered to a multiplicity of service users, so although there may be some transferable assessment skills, knowledge and values, the practice of assessment will differ depending on an assortment of circumstances.

The aim of this book is to provide an initial generic introduction to social work assessment that can be applied to a variety of situations. It would be possible to write a textbook about assessment of children, or assessment of disabled children, and many other very specific service user groups. It would be possible to write a textbook about assessment from one theoretical perspective, such as psychoanalytic or cognitive behavioural. The approach of this book must inevitably make it a general introductory textbook, but I hope you will find it helpful as such.

Style

There is an old joke referring to Sherlock Holmes and Doctor Watson on a camping trip. In the middle of the night Holmes awakes and nudges his faithful friend. 'Watson, look up at the sky and tell me what you see.' Watson replies, 'I see millions of stars.' 'What does that tell you, Watson?' 'Well . . . astronomically, it tells me that there are millions of galaxies and potentially billions of planets. Horologically, I deduce that the time is approximately a quarter past three. Meteorologically, I suspect that we will have a beautiful day tomorrow. Why, what does it tell you?' Holmes is silent for a moment, then says, 'Watson, someone has stolen our tent.'

At the risk of spoiling a good laugh by analysing the joke, there is a danger that we over-interpret matters academically and theoretically, when a simple truth may be staring us in the face. When I read coursework assignments from social work students on the degree programme, I sometimes wish that they would write them in less complex and elaborate language, which for some reason they seem to believe is required, and put forward sound ideas in a simpler style that goes to the point of what they are trying to say. In this book I will myself endeavour not to be obscure and ambiguous in a complex theoretical style, but to put forward fundamental ideas in unadorned language. Social work assessment involves clear interpersonal communication between a social worker and the person being assessed, so to 'practise what I preach' I will aim to adopt that style in my communication with you throughout this book.

Book structure

Having acknowledged above the variety of social work situations that involve assessment, a whole chapter, Chapter 1, will be devoted to discussing *What is assessment?* We will explore its purpose, issues involved in gathering and analysing information, and look at different types of assessment in social work practice.

Chapters 2, 3 and 4 will review the skills, knowledge and values social workers need to undertake assessments. Chapter 2 will explore basic interpersonal and good communication skills used in social work, applying them particularly to assessment situations.

Having said above that textbooks could be written from one theoretical perspective, Chapter 3 will introduce you to a variety of underpinning theories by presenting a number of them briefly. Some can help you understand human nature, while others point to ways of moving on to social work intervention, following assessment. There will be suggestions for further reading and ways of taking theoretical ideas further. Chapter 4 will highlight the professional value base underpinning assessment, emphasising the importance that any assessments you conduct should be undertaken in a manner that respects the humanity of those being assessed, does not assume anything in advance and does not pre-judge other people or discriminate against them.

Every social work assessment to some extent involves assessing risks, as well as needs and people's circumstances. Because of this, Chapter 5 will explore issues related to the assessment of risk and whether risk can, or should be, entirely avoided in what some have termed our 'risk society'. If social workers work towards helping people cope independently with their lives, we must allow service users to face some personal risks. Part of this chapter will also involve exploring the assessment of risk that some people can pose towards others and themselves.

Chapters 6, 7 and 8 will be devoted to applying social work assessment to some broad statutory practice areas and service user groups. This will place generic assessment ideas in the context of government agendas, policies, initiatives and legislation. Chapter 6 will review Children's Services, Chapter 7 Adult Services and Community Care and Chapter 8 Mental Health.

A final conclusion will summarise what we have covered, reinforce some important learning points, make a few concluding remarks and encourage you to continue reading and looking at further sources of information.

Using a textbook

You should not be expected to read a textbook from cover to cover as you do a novel. Although textbooks have a structure, as outlined above, the chapters cover different, related, complementary and sometimes overlapping areas. It is acceptable to go directly to one chapter because you want to look at that topic and read all of it or the most appropriate and relevant sections, which will be introduced with headings and subheadings. Each *chapter summary* and/or the *introduction* may help you understand what that chapter is about and whether it is one to tackle immediately. You do not have to read a textbook's chapters in the order in which they appear in the book.

Learning features

This textbook, as all in this series, has other additional features that will help you interact with the material, rather than just read. There will be practise-based examples and *case studies* to illustrate how ideas about assessment are applied to practice situations. Most of these are based on actual work with service users from practice experience gathered over the years.

The textbook also has occasional *reflection points* and *activities*. Pause at these and use them as instructed. *Reflection points* will encourage you to think about issues, often to reflect about yourself, before you read on. It may be an idea to write down your thoughts for future reference. *Activities* are simple exercises that help you consider aspects of what is being presented and experience it for yourself. When you move on, each of these is followed by a *comment* that helps you compare your thinking and findings to points made and guidance given by the textbook.

Another feature is *research summaries.* They briefly outline examples of relevant research, which help us understand that assessment practice can be based on empirical evidence (gathered from observation, experience or experiment) and not merely based on *a priori* (literally 'from the former' or independent of experience) theorising.

At the start of each chapter there is a section entitled *Achieving your Social Work Degree.* These sections list the National Occupational Standards for Social Work most relevant to the chapter. You are assessed against these on practice placements, so it is important to get to know them well, what they mean, and what might constitute evidence to show that you have met them. They are followed by social work subject benchmark statements from the Quality Assurance Agency for Higher Education. Degree programmes have to show that they adhere to these, in addition to other requirements, when their degrees are validated, so again, it is important that you become familiar with requirements that apply to areas of social work.

At the end of each chapter there are *further reading* suggestions. Since this is an introductory textbook, it is important that when you choose chapters to look through you are then able to pursue those topics further through more specific reading and, in some cases, relevant websites.

Terminology

I have already in this introduction used the term *service user* and it may be worth commenting on that choice. The term is sometimes shortened to just *user.* The organisation *Shaping our Lives* describes itself as a *National User Network* with one of its aims being *to give a shared voice to user controlled organisations.* Many social workers still use the term *clients,* as it has been used for many years within social care and social work circles. Other terms are explicitly or implicitly applied. In the managerialist culture of local authorities and other large organisations, service users are often considered *customers* or *consumers* of a service with rights to participate in service planning and to complain if the service is unsatisfactory.

Language is important and terms already mentioned are labels we give to the people for whom we work, at times with very little if any consultation with them. Language carries meaning and can have positive and negative connotations. The term *people who use services* is one favoured by a number of current influential bodies, such as the General Social Care Council (GSCC), the Care Quality Commission (CQC) and government departments. In a call for people who have experience of using care services to influence the way services are inspected and reports written, the CQC is advertising for people to become an *expert by experience.* The term *experts by experience* has been adopted by some specific groups, particularly disabled people. Having said all this, we must not forget that local authorities also have a statutory obligation to assess *carers* – those who provide unpaid care usually to a relative but occasionally someone such as a close friend, so social workers assess them as well.

While being fully behind the principle that people with whom we work should participate as fully as possible with us, I have decided to use the term *service user* mainly throughout this book as it is short (although not as short as *user*, which I personally dislike) and refers to the person who is being assessed as in need of services that they go on to use. You should assume that when I use the term *service user* it includes *carers* as well. When there is a need to emphasise additional characteristics I use other terms.

I also mainly use the term *social worker* throughout this book. Practitioners that have undertaken a social work qualifying degree programme and are registered with the GSCC mostly call themselves *social workers* when working with children and families and in mental health. Those that work within adult services and community care, with older persons, learning and physically disabled adults and others, tend to use the term *care manager.* Most local authorities in fact accept persons with qualifications such as nursing and occupational therapy, in addition to social work, as care managers. Government initiatives outlined in Chapter 7 suggest that types of worker, responsibilities, training and qualifications are changing as initiatives develop. In chapters discussing assessment and its transferable skills, knowledge, values and other characteristics, I use the term social worker to denote any practitioner undertaking a social work assessment. When I am referring to more specific areas of work I may use more particular terms for the practitioners involved.

Chapter 1

What is assessment?

A C H I E V I N G   A   S O C I A L   W O R K   D E G R E E

This chapter will help you to meet the following National Occupational Standards:

Key Role 1: Prepare for and work with individuals, families, carers, groups and communities to assess their needs and circumstances.

- Work with individuals, families, carers, groups and communities to help them make informed decisions.
- Assess needs and options to recommend a course of action.

Key Role 3: Support individuals to represent their needs, views and circumstances.

- Advocate with, and on behalf of, individuals, families, carers, groups and communities.

Key Role 5: Manage and be accountable, with supervision and support, for your own social work practice within your organisation.

- Work within multi-disciplinary and multi-organisational teams, networks and systems.

Key Role 6: Demonstrate professional competence in social work practice.

- Research, analyse, evaluate and use current knowledge of best social work practice.

This chapter will also introduce you to the following academic standards as set out in the social work subject benchmark statement.

5.1.4 Social work theory.

Models and methods of assessment, including factors underpinning the selection and testing of relevant information, the nature of professional judgement and the processes of risk assessment.

5.1.5 The nature of social work practice.

The factors and processes that facilitate effective inter-disciplinary, inter-professional and inter-agency collaboration and partnership.

Problem-solving skills.

5.5.2. Gathering information.

- Gather information from a wide range of sources and by a variety of methods, for a range of purposes. These methods should include electronic searches using the internet, reviews of relevant written materials, face-to-face, written and telephone contact with individuals and groups.
- Take into account differences of viewpoint in gathering information and assess the reliability and relevance of the information gathered.

5.5.3 Analysis and synthesis.

- Analyse information gathered, weighing competing evidence and modifying their viewpoint in light of new information, then relate this information to a particular task, situation or problem.

5.6 Communication skills.
- Listen actively to others, engage appropriately with the life experiences of service users, understand accurately their viewpoint and overcome personal prejudices to respond appropriately to a range of complex personal and interpersonal situations.

5.7 Skills in working with others.
- Consult actively with others, including service users, who hold relevant information or expertise.

Introduction

From your own personal experience, or looking up dictionary definitions, you will probably agree that 'assessment' is usually understood or defined as measuring, evaluating or making judgements about something. In social work the first point of contact between a potential service user and a social worker will involve some assessment. No one can come to a social work organisation or agency and obtain a service on demand. As a social work student you are required to learn about assessment theoretically and to demonstrate competence in assessment skills during practice placements.

REFLECTION POINT

Can you recall experiences when you have been 'assessed' at various points in your life? Examples may include:

- *written and other work (e.g. artwork, projects) assessed at school;*

- *assessment of competence for cycling proficiency or your driving test;*

- *a GP assessing your symptoms and telling you there is little wrong or diagnosing some ill health;*

- *further and higher education assessment of coursework or exams;*

- *suitability for a job assessed at an employment interview.*

If you have experience as a past or current social work student, this will also include:

- *assessment of academic assignments;*

- *assessment of your practice against National Occupational Standards for Social Work.*

Are there some common factors in relation to the above examples?

Recalling when you have experienced similar assessments, how did you feel before, during and after being assessed?

Comment

The common factors in the above examples might include:

- someone is observing you, asking you questions, looking at examples of your work or behaviour;

- as part of being assessed you are giving information or evidence of some sort;

- someone with the responsibility to do so gathers the evidence in an agreed way and assesses it against given standards, expectations or judgements;

- you may or may not agree with the assessment someone makes about you.

Feelings might include:

- apprehension or anxiety before and during assessment;

- these feelings may continue after assessment and might include anticipation and fear if you are waiting for a result;

- you may have been disappointed or, conversely, experienced feelings of accomplishment when you learnt the outcome of an assessment, whether this was immediately after it or whether you had to wait for some time.

Although not exact parallels, there may be some similarities in the above experiences, common factors and feelings with the experiences and feelings of service users when they are the subject of an assessment by a social worker.

What is assessment?

In a guide for learning and teaching assessment in social work, Whittington (2007) writes about the significance of assessment in social work practice and education. He states that

Professional or organisational assessment represents the entry of an intentionally rational and systematic approach to the encounter between a social worker and people seeking help or services, who may be individuals, couples, families, groups or communities.

(Whittington, 2007, p15)

A difficulty is that there is no single agreed definition of social work assessment. Whittington (2007) suggests that there are four types of definition found in textbooks and frameworks:

- processed-focused;

- contingent;

- contestation-focused;

- critical social constructionist.

Process-focused is a rather technical view of assessment providing guidance on what to do, questions to ask and procedures to follow. Local authorities and other organisations provide some of this for their workers.

There are similarities to a process-focus in defining assessment as **contingent**. An important point here is that these definitions suggest assessment is contingent, or dependent, on the type of service being offered, the goals of assessment and the theoretical underpinning used to make sense of assessment.

In defining assessment as **contestation-focused**, the focal point will be on the inevitable conflicts between the needs of the person seeking help or services and the eligibility criteria used by the agency; the social worker's individual idealism and the realism of criteria and finite resources; and the tensions between needs, risks and resources.

A **critical social constructionist** view suggests that the act of assessment involves the construction of meanings; there will be different interpretations of 'need' suggesting that understanding is socially constructed; a social worker may well construe the narrative or story of a potential service user in their own individual way.

All the above approaches inform discussion in this textbook but chapters will encourage you to take a critical approach to considering the skills, knowledge and values necessary for assessment in social work. In addition, you will need to apply what you learn in supervised practice. The different ways of defining assessment point to some of its complexities. Social workers follow GSCC (2004) Codes of Practice, work to National Occupational Standards for Social Work (Skills for Care, 2002) and have a commitment to a professional value base. The International Federation of Social Workers adopted a definition of social work in 2000 that is also used as the Key Purpose of social work in the National Occupational Standards. It describes social work as a profession that *promotes . . . the empowerment and liberation of people to enhance well-being.* It ends by stating that *Principles of human rights and social justice are fundamental to social work.* The wording suggests values leading to accepting people as individuals and enabling them to achieve their goals, advocating for their rights if necessary; in short, being person-centred. However, these ideal values might well be constrained by agency criteria, procedures and the availability of resources. Since the social worker is making professional judgements as part of assessment, it may be difficult for a service user not to feel an imbalance of power. Social workers will be called on to assess risks involved in someone managing on their own or being in a possibly dangerous or harmful situation. The assessment may make the service user feel disempowered. These tensions are explored further in this and other chapters.

As a social worker undertaking assessments you will be required to engage and interact with a service user, gather information, evaluate it and come to a professional conclusion or conclusions. This is not one easily outlined activity but a continuous and at times complex process that can be more or less formal, more or less objective, brief and initial or core and comprehensive.

Informal and formal assessments

There is a sense in which as a social worker you will be continually assessing the situation and circumstances of service users with whom you are working. Asking 'How are you?' is an open invitation for a person to tell you something about themselves there and then. 'How have things been since we last met?' can lead to a review of progress and circumstances since the last meeting. With these and similar appropriate questions you may continue to monitor or assess how plans jointly made with a service user are progressing.

Initially a social worker may be assessing whether someone who has requested help has come to the right agency or organisation and whether their apparent level of need is such that it warrants the agency investing resources on the service user, i.e. whether the person requesting help meets the agency's 'eligibility criteria'. If after an initial assessment a decision is made to proceed, social workers at times undertake very specific 'core' or 'comprehensive' assessments of need based on thorough guidance frameworks and involving the completion of complex forms. As the involvement with a service user continues, there may be points where a social worker makes an assessment of new situations that come to light.

CASE STUDY

Margaret, a local authority care manager, undertook the assessment of 83-year-old Mrs Edith Brown, who is physically frail and has restricted mobility. In consultation with Mrs Brown, Margaret arranged a care package to allow her to remain living on her own with the support of carers from a private agency coming in twice a day to undertake personal care. Edith has extra help and support from a son and daughter, Paul and Norma, who visit her regularly.

There is a requirement that care packages should be monitored and reviewed periodically. During a review meeting Edith told Margaret that Paul is handling her finances but that he has asked whether he can 'borrow' some money from her bank account and she is not too happy about this. When she told him she would like to buy an electrically adjustable riser/recliner armchair, Paul said she didn't have enough money for it, although she thought there was more than the necessary amount in her account.

Comment

The care manager would have to make an assessment to find out about the situation. This is a matter that has arisen after the original assessment that led to the implementation of a care package for Mrs Brown. It is a sensitive area and one to be investigated carefully as it could result in the finding that Mrs Brown's son is misusing her mother's money and financial abuse is taking place.

CASE STUDY

Melissa and Patsy

Susan, a local authority children and families social worker, is supporting Melissa, a single parent with a 13-month-old daughter, Patsy. Patsy has recently started walking. Susan notices bruises on Patsy's face, arms and legs during a visit. On asking about them, Melissa says that Patsy is clumsy and keeps bumping into furniture.

Comment

At this stage in her work with Melissa, Susan has to find out more about the circumstances leading to the bruising, whether they are accidental, and about Melissa's parenting skills. She may do this in partnership with other professionals. Susan will assess the risk that Patsy may be suffering significant harm. Susan is required to do this under legislation and will have her local authority's policies and procedures to follow. This could lead to a professional judgement that Melissa is physically abusing Patsy.

The social work process

Although as suggested by the case studies above, assessment can take place at various points during work with a service user, it is helpful to think of assessment as a starting point in the process of social work. As we saw earlier, social workers must make an assessment before they can decide whether to work with a person, and may then go on to decide how they can work with the person, what to offer, what issues to focus on and what needs to attempt to meet. They will do this initially and continue to make such decisions as work goes on.

What we have explored so far suggests that social work is an ongoing process. It has been described by writers over the years using terms such as *assessment, care planning, implementation and evaluation* (Taylor and Devine, 1993); *assessment, intervention, review, ending and evaluation* (Thompson, 2005); *assessment, planning, intervention, review* (Parker, 2007; Parker and Bradley, 2007).

Sutton (1999) puts forward the mnemonic ASPIRE to illustrate the process of:

- AS – Assessment.
- P – Planning.
- I – Intervention.
- RE – Review and Evaluation.

Connexions personal advisers working with 13 to 19-year-olds use an APIR (Assessment, Planning, Implementation, Review) framework initially published by the then Department for Education and Skills (DfES, 2001).

When a Care Management model of work with adult service users was implemented, the Department of Health published guidance (Department of Health, Social Services Inspectorate, 1991) where the way of working is outlined as a cycle consisting of:

1. Publishing information.
2. Determining the level of assessment (following referral).
3. Assessing need.
4. Care planning.
5. Implementing the care plan.

6. Monitoring.

7. Review.

Although there are slight variations in the number of stages and their descriptions, there is agreement among the above sources that social work (or care management) is a process and that assessment is fundamental to it and a core skill (or a complex integration of skills, knowledge and values).

The social work process has a logical progression but in practice it will almost certainly not be a linear, chronological sequence moving neatly from one stage to another. As suggested by the case studies above, assessment may reveal urgent matters to be dealt with immediately. While initial assessment is taking place a social worker and service user may already start to plan certain courses of action. Intervention with a service user may bring to light pieces of information or behaviour that add to a full assessment of circumstances and developments. Informal and ongoing monitoring and review, or formal periodic reviews and evaluation, may lead to reassessment. All this points to social work being cyclical, ongoing, fluid and dynamic, rather than a linear process. The fluidity and dynamic nature of the process suggests that each component of it will have these characteristics to contribute to the cycle. The stages will not consist of discrete tasks involving a single skill. Thus assessment itself can be seen to fit in as a dynamic process requiring integration of skills, knowledge and values.

Defining assessment

In discussing the history of assessment in social work Milner and O'Byrne (2009), although not offering a formal definition, refer to *gathering information, sifting it carefully and coming up with an 'objective' and 'accurate' conclusion* (p8). In reviewing assessment theories, Coulshed and Orme (2006, p24) describe assessment as

> ... *an ongoing process in which the client or service user participates, the purpose of which is to assist the social worker to understand people in relation to their environment. Assessment is also a basis for planning what needs to be done to maintain, improve or bring about change in the person, the environment or both.*

Parker and Bradley (2007) explore the question of whether assessment in social work is an art or a science as central to the debate about definitions. They propose that if assessment were an art it could *not be limited by definitions, structured questionnaires, checklists or even fully described, rather it would rely on the wisdom and skill of the assessor as refined through experience*. If assessment were a science, *assessments should be open to precise measurement and be practised effectively by following steps outlined in a 'technical manual' of social work*. They conclude:

> *A balanced approach would suggest that social work assessment is both an art and a science since it involves wisdom, skills, appreciation of diversity and systematic applied knowledge In practice.*

(Parker and Bradley, 2007, p4)

Although what follows is not an exhaustive list, it may be helpful to outline some of the expected components of most assessments and move on to reflect on and expand the ideas and concepts to clarify them at this stage.

Assessment will involve:

- gathering and assembling full and accurate information about a service user's circumstances and how these came about;

- analysing information objectively, constructing hypotheses that explain what is happening and what might be done, making professional judgements and coming to accurate conclusions;

- participation by the service user and others (e.g. family) to identify issues and how they might be addressed;

- assessing eligibility for services and level of need;

- gathering information from, sharing information and consulting with colleagues and workers in other agencies;

- using systems to record information accurately.

ACTIVITY **1.1**

How would you go about undertaking each of the components of assessment listed above?

What skills, knowledge and values might help you undertake each activity?

Comment

It may help you to compare your answers to the questions in the above activity box with comments under the six following headings, which relate to each of the bullet points outlining what is involved in assessment.

Gathering information

Many interpersonal and communication skills are involved in gathering information. These will include asking questions of, listening to and entering into discussion with service users and other significant people such as members of the family and others closely connected with the service user. You should not ask random questions or focus on areas you find of personal interest or that you particularly want to follow up. An assessment interview will have a purpose and plan (see Chapter 2).

Pamela Trevithick, in her practice handbook *Social work skills* (Trevithick, 2005), devotes a chapter to *Communication, listening and assessment skills*, interestingly including assessment skills in a chapter about interpersonal communication. She stresses the importance of verbal and non-verbal communication, observation and listening skills, before moving on to assessment, its purpose and features.

To gather information it will help you to have knowledge of the service user group with whom you are working (e.g. children, disabled people, substance misuse, offending behaviour, mental health problems, older persons, etc.). Your communication may have to be adjusted to be appropriate to the service user with whom you are working.

Observation skills are crucial to assessment and gathering information will involve all five human senses (sight, hearing, touch and body sensations, smell, taste). As a social worker you will observe people and their surroundings and notice significant pieces of information through looking carefully about you. You will also hear and read information. You will probably also gather information through means such as sensing the temperature of a house (e.g. cold or over-heated), smelling odours and even using the sense of taste if, for instance, you are offered a drink during a home visit.

CASE STUDY

Dwayne

Charles, a social worker in a community mental health team, is allocated the initial assessment of Dwayne, a 23-year-old single man living with his African-Caribbean parents. On visiting the home Charles experiences a culture shock as everything is so different from his own English traditions. There is loud reggae music and many ornaments and decorations with vibrant red, yellow and green colours. There are strong smells of frying and spices coming from the kitchen. Dwayne is a fast and lively speaker and Charles has to concentrate hard to tune into his accent.

Analysing information objectively

Assessment does not involve merely common sense. Members of the public unaware of the scope and complexities of social work sometimes ask, 'Why do you have to do a three-year degree course to be a social worker?' Does it not just involve helping people?'

Assessment is more than information gathering. The information gathered by the senses is processed by the brain, so you will use cognitive, or intellectual, skills to analyse it using theoretical knowledge and make inferences and judgements. Information may not always be reliable or logical. There may be differences of viewpoint to take into consideration. You will synthesise information from various sources and weigh competing evidence before reaching conclusions.

You will need knowledge of legal duties and powers, policies and procedures. You will need to understand a service user's culture, ethnicity, nationality and socio-economic level. There may be social pressures that impact on the levels of need being assessed. Individuals may feel oppressed, discriminated against and socially excluded with few resources at their disposal to tackle personal circumstances and problems. You will be making an assessment to understand a person in relation to their environment. In analysing information you may make a hypothesis about present circumstances and how they might be improved. In so doing, you will be using the knowledge of underpinning theoretical models and explanations (see Chapter 3). You may need to understand a person's previous experiences that are affecting their current behaviour.

CASE STUDY

Melissa and Patsy

Susan the social worker has established a good relationship with Melissa so is able to openly and honestly ask about Patsy's bruises. Susan is guided by her local authority's procedures. In talking to Melissa and Patsy it helps her to have knowledge and be aware of Patsy's level of cognitive development and her attachment to her mother Melissa. This will inform the type of questions Susan asks.

Milner and O'Byrne (2009, pp61, 62) propose five stages in the process of making assessments:

1. Preparation.

2. Data collection.

3. Weighing the data.

4. Analysing the data.

5. Utilising the analysis.

In weighing the data, social workers will be using underpinning knowledge and theoretical models. The writers suggest that in the fourth stage social workers will *Identify theoretical perspectives and use them to gain depth of analysis. Develop more than one hypothesis... Test the explanations for possible theoretical 'fit'.*

Service user participation

Social work assessment is not a 'diagnosis' of problems by an expert but a joint exercise where the service user is an expert by experience. Social work is about working with people to assess, plan, tackle and review their needs or problems. So assessment must involve the service user in gathering information and making sense of it. There is a danger that a social worker may too readily assume issues or start thinking about what help might be offered, based on the social worker's previous experience and on resources available, before fully exploring the service user's circumstances and perceptions.

Assessment will involve discussion to identify issues and the use of skills to enable a service user to reflect on their situation. In addition, a social worker may enter into discussion with members of the service user's family and other key people to make a full and rounded assessment. Since the social worker has the responsibility to make the assessment and the service user is being assessed, there can be a power imbalance that makes the service user feel oppressed. There is a need to look for ways to equalise the relationship and for the assessment to be a partnership between social worker and service user (see Chapter 4).

CASE STUDY

Dwayne

After a first visit, Charles looked up on the internet information about African-Caribbean culture generally and specifically about the Rastafarian faith, worship and symbols that Dwayne talked about in their first meeting. This helped Charles enter into further discussion with Dwayne and understand him, including his background and beliefs, much better. Charles also talked to Dwayne's parents about their settling into this country and Dwayne's early years.

Charles agreed to meet Dwayne at an African-Caribbean community centre he attends regularly and began to understand Dwayne's explanation that some of his behaviour can seem bizarre to professionals but is in keeping with his culture and customs.

Recent years have seen a growing realisation and commitment in social work that the voice of service users needs to be heard and that their participation in all aspects of service planning and delivery is in keeping with professional social work values. Parallel and related to this has been the development of the service user movement, or movements, exemplified by groups of people coming together for support, advocacy and campaigning such as survivors of the mental health system and disabled people. The motto *Nothing about us without us* has been used by the disability movement and has become the title of publications such as a book about the oppression of disabled people (Charlton, 1998) in which the author states he first came across the expression in South Africa in 1993; a Department of Health strategy for learning disability written in collaboration with a Service Users Advisory Group (Department of Health, 2001b); and an international report examining the involvement of people who use illegal drugs in tackling the problem (Jürgens, 2008).

The sentiments encapsulated by the motto apply to social work assessment. In assessing service users, nothing about them should be uncovered, sifted, discussed, concluded and written down without their participation and knowledge. Further interesting developments related to service user perspectives concerning assessment are ideas such as 'user-led', 'user-defined' and 'self-assessment'. These will be explored further in subsequent chapters.

Assessing eligibility for services

Social workers undertake assessments as a representative of the agency or organisation for which they work. They are bound by the agency's remit, policies and procedures. Assessment takes place when someone first makes contact with an agency. This might be through a referral by another professional or as a self-referral. The initial task, therefore, will be to gather enough information to decide whether the person meets the eligibility criteria for that agency.

One conclusion might be that the person has come, or has been referred, to the wrong place. A social worker in an organisation or team dealing with people with mental health problems may explain that they cannot offer a service to someone with a learning disability. In times of finite resources and limited budgets, social workers in local authorities and other agencies may make an assessment that the person's circumstances are such that a service cannot be offered as they do not meet the tight eligibility band or severity level. Local authority children and families teams may be required to devote resources mainly to child protection investigations and not be able to offer help to a family that needs a lower level of support. A care manager might work for a local authority that only offers services to adults assessed as having substantial or critical needs and not if the needs are moderate or low. (These issues are discussed further in Chapters 6 and 7.)

Collaboration with other professionals

Social workers may need to, with permission, seek information from other professionals such as doctors, teachers, health visitors, nursery workers, colleagues in voluntary organisations (e.g. day and neighbourhood centres), community psychiatric nurses, psychologists, occupational therapists and many more.

Social workers do not gather information alone but are increasingly required to work in cooperation with other professionals in multi-agency partnerships. Public inquiries into tragedies have highlighted:

- unclear accountability;

- poor communication;

- poor coordination of services;

- lack of collaboration and information sharing between agencies.

When things go wrong, social workers attract criticism and negative media coverage. Quinney (2006, p22) points out that *In the current context, collaborative practice has been widely promoted as a solution for addressing shortcomings and failures in public services, including the social work, health, education, youth work and housing sectors.*

Social workers undertake assessments working in partnership with agencies such as the police, hospitals and other health services, SureStart, Connexions, and a variety of voluntary agencies. This can be difficult, as Sharkey (2000) has pointed out, due to the:

- number of organisations involved;

- different structures making communication difficult;

- different budgets and financial arrangements;

- geographical boundaries;

- weak legislative and policy guidance.

As a social worker you will need to share information with professionals from different backgrounds, training, professional and organisational cultures, using their own jargon and, to some extent, having different values. Health workers may use a 'medical model' to understand a person's condition, whereas a social worker will be more likely to be informed by a 'social model' that highlights how society can discriminate against individuals due to their disability, mental ill health or other condition.

In recent years the government has attempted to strengthen legislative and policy guidance, the last point in Sharkey's list, requiring multi-agency collaboration (as will be explored in Chapters 6, 7 and 8). However, this also puts pressure on social workers to spend time on administrative tasks.

CASE STUDY

Melissa and Patsy

Through discussion with Melissa, Susan is aware that Melissa has contact with her GP and a health visitor attached to the GP practice. Patsy has started attending a nursery two mornings a week. They had previously talked about the possibility of Susan referring Melissa to a local family centre run by a voluntary organisation as it offers a parenting skills group. Melissa was in agreement and thought the group might be useful.

Susan realises she is not making an assessment in isolation, but that she has to communicate with other professionals and agencies, gather information collaboratively, coordinate help being offered and share information.

As a social worker you should have available professional consultation and not make judgements alone. Inquiries into tragedies have criticised lack of management supervision and the keeping of supervision notes. One of the Victoria Climbié enquiry recommendations, for instance, was that *Directors of social services must ensure that the work of staff working directly with children is regularly supervised* (Laming, 2003). In addition, you will have specialists available to call on such as child protection and adult protection coordinators and legal advisers. Consulting others with specialist knowledge within your agency and other professionals is part of making professional judgements and deciding how to proceed.

Systems to record information accurately

Social workers use assessment tools and frameworks and are required to keep a careful record of what they have done and what they have found. The importance of having a careful record of assessment can be argued in terms of:

- assembling the information gathered;
- clarity and objectivity;
- facilitating service user participation;
- recording eligibility;

- recording shortfalls and absence of services;

- sharing information with other professionals;

- its usefulness for supervision purposes;

- ensuring accountability;

- 'covering' the worker for work done;

- providing continuity when workers change or dealing with a case in a worker's absence.

Some of the above items are from an original summary of the multi-purpose nature of record keeping in Coulshed (1991) that is used by Trevithick (2005) to review record-keeping skills. I have adapted the list and added items in keeping with the previous discussion.

Social workers often voice frustration that so much of their work involves adminis-trative paperwork. The trends towards managerialism, responding to bureaucratic regulation and contributing to data-based reviews can make recording systems unpopular. Public and management inquiries when things go wrong often suggest safeguards that involve further recording to show that procedures are being followed. Local authority children's services currently are required to use an Integrated Chil-dren's System (ICS) of computer data recording that many social workers criticise as being more helpful for monitoring performance measures than helping in the analysis of a family's and children's needs. At the time of writing a national Social Work Task Force is making recommendations for improvements.

However, the above is a positive list of reasons for recording information accurately and part of your professional practice will be to manage the balance of face-to-face contact with service users and keeping a record of work undertaken to help the social work process.

The purpose of assessment

Not assessing accurately with participation from service users would lead to services being offered without considering what specific needs you are attempting to meet. You would offer an 'off the peg' rather than 'tailor made' service and, at worse, you would be offering 'one size fits all' services because they are on the agency's 'peg' without the customer being able to choose one that is at least the nearest fit or style. As Coulshed and Orme (2006) state in the definition we considered earlier in this chapter, assessment will lead you to *understand people in relation to their environ-ment* and it is a basis for planning helpful intervention aimed at bringing about change as agreed with the service user.

Having said that, we acknowledged that as a social worker you will also be working to an agency remit and have statutory powers and duties. Assessment cannot be under-taken in isolation from these considerations. We already saw earlier that social work assessment will involve an initial decision, based on eligibility criteria, whether a service can be offered at all by your agency. In addition, there may be times when, as a statutory social worker, you have to undertake a risk assessment and assess a situation or a person's behaviour against legal safeguards. A children and families social worker may have to act on the local authority's duty to investigate whether a child is, in the words of section 47 of the Children Act 1989, *suffering, or is likely to suffer, significant harm*. A social worker in a Community Mental Health team may be involved in a decision as to whether a service user suffering mental ill health needs to be detained in hospital if he or she is a danger to themselves or others.

Such assessments may be against the wishes of a service user and pose the social worker an ethical dilemma. The two examples just mentioned are extreme cases involving removal of a child from home or committing someone to hospital possibly against their will. But even in other circumstances social workers will not always be able to respond to service users' wants. It is important then for the social worker to explain reasons why something is not possible and to keep the service user informed at all times. The assessment process will then be a joint one, ideally a partnership with the service user. As a social worker you will be working to professional values, including respecting and promoting each person as an individual, their independence and quality of life, while protecting them from harm. You will be aware of your own values, prejudices, ethical dilemmas and conflicts of interest and their implications on practice (see Chapter 4). The above considerations may make more sense by acknowledging that social workers can play a number of roles.

Social work roles

ACTIVITY 1.2

List personal and social roles you play in your life.

List roles a social worker may play.

Comment

We all play personal and social roles in our lives – daughter/son, mother/father, aunt/uncle, friend, employee, member of social group(s). You may have listed others. These roles influence our identity and behaviour. The roles may occasionally be in conflict and can change over time, but they are played by one person.

Higham (2006) argues *that social workers must practise multiple roles in order to deal with complex situations* and suggests that *the use of self can help them avoid an unwitting misuse of power by developing more self-awareness.* She proposes *Professional roles that social workers adopt include a versatile and flexible range:*

- *planner*

- *assessor*

- *evaluator*

- *counsellor*

- *supporter*

- *advocate*

- *manager.*

One way of looking at this is that as a social worker you will undertake different roles related to the social work process – 'assessor'; 'planner'; roles related to intervention such as 'helper', 'supporter', 'care manager'; and 'reviewer' or 'evaluator'. It could be argued that there are roles missing in Higham's list. In safeguarding individuals social workers can at times play roles that could be interpreted as 'agent of social control' or a 'social police' role. These roles might apply when as a social worker you are making an assessment that someone needs to be protected from harm to themselves or others.

Contestation-focused and, even more so, critical social constructionist definitions mentioned earlier in this chapter question how objective and accurate conclusions arrived at in assessments can be. In whose opinion or judgement are the conclusions reached, particularly if service users disagree with them? The question whether social work assessment is a science, leading to precise measurement, arises again. Assessments concerning human nature, relationships, social situations and circumstances involve making qualitative judgements more than measuring quantities. In interacting with the person being assessed, social workers may come to conclusions that can be seen as a social construction, and the language, discourse or narrative they use can define situations or label those involved. We touched on some of these issues earlier when considering service user participation as part of what assessment involves.

REFLECTION POINT

If you are or have been a student on a social work degree programme, consider your relationship with your practice teacher/assessor during assessed placements.

How helpful did you find their verbal and written feedback after direct observations of your practice?

How open and honest were you able to be when discussing evidence of your competence?

Since they had the responsibility to recommend a Pass or Fail by the end of the placement, did you feel disempowered in any way?

Comment

These reflections may help you consider the relationship between a service user and the social worker who is undertaking their assessment.

As in the personal examples that you considered at the start of this chapter, the knowledge and skill of the 'assessor' can be perceived as power, making the person assessed feel disempowered, at the mercy of the assessor with no contribution to make other than having provided some of the information that needed to be gathered.

Are social workers' assessments objectively made with reference to external principles and expectations rather than the standards of the service users themselves? There is a danger of a 'them and us' approach – social workers belonging to a professional group of people entitled to assess other people's problems but not having any of their own.

In a critical approach to social work, Fook (2002, p117) points out that the process and criteria of assessment are

> *integral to the process of defining service users in disempowered ways, and of defining problems as the responsibility of disempowered rather than dominant groups; and of defining those with problems as separate from or different to dominant groups who do not have problems. Assessment discourses, and the ways in which problems are defined and labeled, are thereby integral to the process and structures which preserve dominant power relations.*

To guard against oppressive practice that disempowers service users, Fook suggests taking into account a number of ideas.

1. Problematic situations will involve a number of complex, competing and contradictory factors.

2. A professional narrative may be constructed and reconstructed as relationships with service users change and new information emerges.

3. Existing labels and categories may need to be resisted.

4. The possibility of constructing an 'assessment narrative' that favours the service user.

5. Creation of more open-ended service user identities and problem categories or definitions, which recognise the influence of changing contexts.

This takes us back to considering and accepting:

- assessment as a fluid and dynamic process which is part of an overall cyclical, ongoing social work process;

- the importance of full participation by service users in their assessments;

- a common humanity between social worker and service user;

- the use of underpinning theoretical knowledge, which may be based on research undertaken in a scientific tradition;

- the use of wisdom and skill by the social worker;

- adherence to professional social work values.

C H A P T E R   S U M M A R Y

This chapter has introduced you to assessment in social work as a crucial but complex, difficult-to-define activity. We saw that it is a starting point in social work but that it continues as a fluid and dynamic ongoing process integrated within the 'assessment, planning, intervention and review' social work cyclical process. There are points during a social worker's involvement with a service user when a further assessment or reassessment needs to take place.

Some of the complexity arises from the fact that assessment can be ongoing and informal, or specific and formal. It can be an initial assessment or a comprehensive 'core' assessment. It has elements of art and science; it involves a number of activities, skills, knowledge and values.

One of the main messages of this chapter has been that service users are central to social work assessment and must be involved at every stage of it.

FURTHER READING

Milner, J and O'Byrne, P (2009) *Assessment in social work.* 3rd edition. Basingstoke: Palgrave Macmillan.
This comprehensive textbook explores assessment with its value base and underpinning theoretical models. Various chapters review conceptual frameworks or theoretical maps to make sense of assessment.

Parker, J and Bradley, G (2010) *Social work practice: Assessment, planning, intervention and review.* 3rd edition. Exeter: Learning Matters.
The writers provide a clear and systematic review of the social work process, with particular emphasis on assessment and assessment tools. Chapters 1 and 2 are devoted to assessment.

Walker, S and Beckett, C (2004) *Social work assessment and intervention.* Lyme Regis: Russell House Publishing.
This book discusses many value issues. It addresses National Occupational Standards for Social Work, General Social Care Council (GSCC) requirements and the relationship between assessment and intervention.

Chapter 2
Skills needed in assessment

This chapter will help you meet the following National Occupational Standards:

Key Role 1: Prepare for, and work with individuals, families, carers, groups and communities to assess their needs and circumstances.

- Work with individuals, families, carers, groups and communities to help them make informed decisions.
- Assess needs and options to recommend a course of action.

Key Role 2: Plan, carry out, review and evaluate social work practice with service users and other professionals.

- Interact with individuals, families, carers, groups and communities to achieve change and development and to improve life opportunities.
- Address behaviour which presents a risk to individuals, families, carers, groups and communities.

Key Role 6: Demonstrate professional competence in social work practice.

- Work within agreed standards of social work practice and ensure own professional development.

It will also introduce you to the following academic standards as set out in the social work subject benchmark statement:

5.1.5 The nature of social work practice.

- The nature and characteristics of skills associated with effective practice, both direct and indirect, with a range of service users and in a variety of settings including group-care.

Problem-solving skills.

5.5.1 Managing problem-solving activities.

- Think logically and systematically.
- Apply ethical principles and practices critically in planning problem-solving activities.
- Plan a sequence of actions to achieve specified objectives.

5.5.2 Gathering information.

- Gather information from a wide range of sources and by a variety of methods, for a range of purposes. These methods should include electronic searches using the internet, reviews of relevant written materials, face-to-face, written and telephone contact with individuals and groups.
- Take into account differences of viewpoint in gathering information and assess the reliability and relevance of the information gathered.

5.5.3 Analysis and synthesis.

- Assess human situations, taking into account a variety of factors (including the views of participants, theoretical concepts, research evidence, legislation and organisational policies and procedures).

- Analyse information gathered, weighing competing evidence and modifying their viewpoint in light of new information, then relate this information to a particular task, situation or problem.
- Consider specific factors relevant to social work practice (such as risk, rights, cultural differences and linguistic sensitivities, responsibilities to protect vulnerable individuals and legal obligations).
- Synthesise information and lines of reasoning and sustain detailed argument at length and over time.
- Employ understanding of human agency at the macro (societal), mezzo (organisational and community) and micro (inter- and intra-personal) levels.
- Analyse and take account of the impact of inequality and discrimination in work with people in particular contexts and problem situations.

5.5.4 Intervention and evaluation.

- Build and sustain purposeful relationships with people and organisations in community-based, and inter-professional contexts including group-care.

5.6 Communication skills.

- Make effective contact with individuals and organisations for a range of objectives, by verbal, paper-based and electronic means.
- Clarify and negotiate the purpose of such contacts and the boundaries of their involvement.
- Listen actively to others, engage appropriately with the life experiences of service users, understand accurately their viewpoint and overcome personal prejudices to respond appropriately to a range of complex personal and interpersonal situations.
- Use both verbal and non-verbal cues to guide interpretation.
- Identify and use opportunities for purposeful and supportive communication with service users within their everyday living situations.
- Communicate effectively across potential barriers resulting from differences (for example, in culture, language and age).

5.7 Skills in working with others.

- Involve users of social work services in ways that increase their resources, capacity and power to influence factors affecting their lives.
- Consult actively with others, including service users, who hold relevant information or expertise.
- Develop effective helping relationships and partnerships with other individuals, groups and organisations that facilitate change.
- Act with others to increase social justice by identifying and responding to prejudice, institutional discrimination and structural inequality.
- Act within a framework of multiple accountability (for example, to agencies, the public, service users and others).
- Challenge others when necessary, in ways that are most likely to produce positive outcomes.

Introduction

This chapter will review and explore skills needed by social workers when undertaking assessments. It will highlight the complexity of interpersonal communication as part of professional social work, even though communicating with others is something we may feel comes naturally as we have been doing it throughout life. We will consider a number of specific skills and how to use them in a variety of situations.

Although it may seem rather basic, a starting point is to be prepared to listen to the person you are going to assess. When the current three-year social work degree qualification was being developed the Department of Health commissioned focus groups of service users and carers to seek their views about the future of social work training (Barnes, 2002). A key message was that *social workers must have skills in listening, counselling, assessing, case managing and finding practical ways to help service users (p5). Listen and learn from us* is a plea that comes through repeatedly whenever service users and carers are asked about their expectations of social workers (Levin, 2004).

At the end of TV interviews on location, it is common to film some independent reaction shots of the interviewer adopting a listening pose, concentrating and nodding – 'noddies' or 'noddy shots' in TV jargon. This footage is then edited into the tape prior to transmission so that while the interviewee is talking there will be a few seconds cutaway to seeing the interviewer attentively 'listening'. However, they are shots of a professional TV interviewer 'pretending' to listen through ritualistic nods at given points during the interview!

This gives some idea of what listening 'looks like' but it does not throw light on what is involved in actively listening to someone. When you are interacting with someone to undertake an assessment you are processing large amounts of information. You may be preoccupied with personal matters. You may still be reflecting on a significant statement that the other person has made when they have moved on to other topics. As a social work student you might sometimes be thinking about what to say next. You may adopt a 'noddy shot' pose while your mind is processing conflicting and distracting information.

Seden (2005, p22) points out that communication is *an interactive process involving the giving, receiving and checking out of meaning.*

REFLECTION POINT

Think of situations when you have approached someone (such as a college or university tutor, a supervisor or manager at work, your GP, a financial adviser) about a matter important to you.

Can you think of a time when you went away disappointed, frustrated or even angry because the person you saw did not seem to understand your concerns and responded to you in an unhelpful way?

Can you think of a time when you felt satisfied, having had a fair hearing and appropriate responses?

List what made each of the two examples in one case a negative and in the other a positive experience. What responses did you find unhelpful or helpful? What personal qualities and skills did the persons you thought of lack or show?

Comment

The negative example may have included the setting for the interaction. Was it noisy with distractions and other people about who could overhear? Did someone representing authority sit opposite you across a desk in an intimidating way?

Negative personal qualities may include a closed mind, overpowering presence or someone putting their own interpretations on your concerns. The person may have been vague, lacking knowledge about matters important to you. Poor skills could include being distracted, not attending and listening, bombarding you with questions about what they wanted to know and not focusing on your concerns.

The positive example may have included a setting with no interruptions or distractions and perhaps the seating arrangement and the person's body posture giving you the message that they were paying full attention.

Positive personal qualities may include accepting you and your concerns and trying to understand issues from your point of view. The person may have shown knowledge about matters that concerned you. Skills could include listening carefully, and asking questions that allowed you to say why you came to see them and to clarify your own thinking.

What is a skill?

In the above activity you may have reflected on the difference between personal qualities and skills. We at times refer to positive qualities a person may have, such as being genuine, interested in people, sensitive, empathetic. This relates to and is part of who we are, our nature. Personal qualities are shaped and influenced by our upbringing and culture; our personal and professional value base underpins them.

Like riding a bicycle or typing, skills involve behaviour that we can learn and improve. So we can consider interpersonal communication and assessment skills that we may already have to some extent but that we can add to, practise and enhance. Moss (2008, p101) points out that

> *in people-work of various kinds all that we really have to offer to someone else is ourselves: our toolkit, if you like, is how we relate to the person who comes to us – in short – our communication skills. Whereas a car mechanic would be lost without a box of spanners and an electronic diagnostic machine, and a dentist without the range of drills, 'prodders' and fillings, people-workers are only effective when they have developed skills to work with the other person in a professional human way.*

Hearing, attending and non-verbal communication

Assessments in social work are best carried out in a setting where you can clearly hear what others are saying. If it is in a person's home you need to consider what room to use and where to sit, balancing the service user's choice with conditions leading to good communication. You could ask that a TV be turned off. If in your workplace it is important that you have a suitable room where there will be no interruptions or distractions. Wherever the assessment takes place you may have to ask to see a service user alone, at least for part of the time.

CASE STUDY

A GP referred a couple, Iris and Ray, both in their 80s, to a local care management team. Ray was experiencing increasing mobility problems and his forgetfulness and confusion suggested dementia, which was being assessed. Iris was finding it difficult to care for her husband. Care manager Adelle called on them to make an initial assessment. A niece was also there. It was not possible to move large and heavy armchairs in the lounge and the seating arrangement was not ideal for an interview. Adelle found Ray to have hearing and short-term memory loss, which made communication with him difficult. She had to make sure she turned round on the settee to face Roy and involve him by asking questions directly to him, then turn round again and ask Iris questions. The niece seemed more used to talking with them and it was tempting at times to communicate through her, but Adelle avoided this as much as possible. Adelle asked if she could have a few minutes alone with Ray, so Iris and her niece went to the kitchen to make a cup of tea. Adelle moved to an armchair opposite Ray and was able to engage with him better.

Paying someone full attention will show that you are physically and psychologically with them. Egan (2007, p76) puts forward the mnemonic SOLER to illustrate the non-verbal attention involved in *the skill of physically tuning in*:

S – facing someone **squarely**, both metaphorically and physically, to indicate involvement;

O – adopting an **open**, non-defensive posture. It can be a sign that you are open to the service user;

L – **leaning** slightly forward towards the other person(s) to show interest;

E – maintaining good **eye contact**;

R – staying relatively **relaxed** or natural.

The extreme of any of them would not be good practice.

Egan (2007, p72) writes about *turn taking* as one of the requirements for true dialogue. As a social worker you will gather information about your service user and will base your assessment on what you *come to understand through the give-and-take of the dialogue*. You will be misusing power if you dictate the turn taking, interrupting and controlling areas you particularly want to know about. Such imbalance in communication can be equated with what Schirato and Yell (2000) called *asymmetry of power*, a term that has been associated with international relationships and clashes of cultures. In an assessment interview it is preferable for the service user to have more time to talk than the social worker.

Active listening

You should not only be listening attentively but also, through responses, make sure the other person is aware that you are listening. Some of the responses will be non-verbal, such as nodding. In addition, it can help to respond to the other person with 'minimal encouragers' such as 'mmm . . .' and 'yes'. Brief 'prompts' can also encourage a person to say more – short statements such as 'tell me more' or repeating a significant word that the person has included in a statement.

A response to 'I'm just fed up with my mother, she's always telling me what to do' can be 'always?' This one word may help the person reflect on the intensity of what they said, consider how they feel about their mother and explore the perception that she is constantly dictating what they should do.

Reflecting, paraphrasing and summarising

These are interlinked and overlapping skills that can be used particularly in assessment to seek feedback to check that you have understood the other person by reflecting back the content of what someone is saying. This can be preceded by 'let me check that I got this right' or 'so what you are saying is . . .' and paraphrasing or summarising what the person has said.

Paraphrasing is conveying the meaning of what a person has said in different but accurate words. The term 'paraphrase' has been used in literature when someone rewrites a complex account in simpler language while conveying the same meaning. Thus there are paraphrases of Shakespeare's plays or of the Bible that simplify the language but still have the basic essence of the original sources.

ACTIVITY 2.1

Paula and Denise
Below are alternative responses at one point of an account by Paula, a 24-year-old mother talking to Denise, a children and families referral team duty officer.
Which one do you think is most appropriate? Would you make a different response?

P: . . . Sam, he's my eldest, he's 7, is not doing very well at school and some welfare woman from the school contacted me to say he's been fighting and swearing. He's been really mouthy at home recently, he can be a little bugger at times, and I've noticed money missing from my purse. Kelly the younger one, who's 4, is easier to cope with but lately she won't do as she's told. I think she's copying Sam.

Response 1
D: So there is a lot for you to cope with . . .

Response 2
D: So Sam's aggressive behaviour may be affecting his schoolwork and both of them, Sam and now Kelly, are disobeying you at home . . .

Response 3
What would be your response?

Comment

There is no one correct response, although some are better than others. Response 1 shows concern for Paula and it could prompt her to speak more about how she is coping and feeling. Response 2 may lead to Paula saying whether she agrees Sam's behaviour is aggressive and considers the children are disobeying her. This may enable Denise to ask more about the children's behaviour and Paula's parenting skills to help her initial assessment. In Response 3 you may have referred to the children's behaviour, the school or found another appropriate way of reflecting and/or paraphrasing the situation that faces Paula. It would be unhelpful to respond in a way that reflected your interest, unrelated to the issues Paula has just raised.

Summarising is another way to check your understanding and whether or not you have grasped someone's meaning. If you summarise facts correctly the service user can be reassured that you have listened; if you have not understood fully the service user can correct you. This is in keeping with the aim of involving service users in their assessment. The skill can be used to summarise understanding at given points, and at the end of a session.

As well as reflecting back factual content, there is a skill in reflecting back feelings. It can be helpful to identify feelings and reflect mixed emotions. This will help the service user become more aware of them and demonstrates that you have understood them.

Using phrases such as 'you sound scared' or 'you seem angry' or questions like 'are you disappointed about this?' are ways of checking that you are getting the whole message when gathering and assembling full and accurate information about a service user's circumstances.

Personal qualities

We considered earlier the difference between personal qualities and skills. Another of the key messages from service users and carers' focus groups (Barnes, 2002, p5) was that *social workers must have personal qualities of warmth, empathy and understanding*. In what has become a classic work in understanding personality and human relationships, Carl Rogers (1961) put forward three personal qualities essential to a person-centred approach in psychotherapy, counselling or being 'helpful' to others.

The first one is **empathy**, arguably the most important quality in helpful and therapeutic listening. It involves understanding a person's circumstances and concerns as if you are that person rather than arriving at your own perceptions filtered through your individual frame of reference, thus understanding what someone else's personal experience means to them. It is important that empathy is accurate and that you are able to communicate this to the service user. You can use skills to check that your understanding is accurate and show empathy through reflecting content and feelings, paraphrasing and summarising.

In exploring counselling skills used in social work, Miller (2006, p40) takes this further by suggesting that

As we learn to stay with a service user's frame of reference, we can develop the capacity not just to hear single statements made but to capture the essence of what is being communicated in total. We can offer what we think we have heard but has not been voiced, such as, 'you sound as if you feel totally helpless', in a way that is both uncertain and open for confirmation or clarification from the service user. The service user takes the lead in the direction of the conversation.

Seden (2005, p20) stresses the importance of *recognising the other's way of communicating.* You have to respect their values and beliefs.

Meanings must be carefully checked and in each exchange care needs to be taken to be aware of, and reduce, the blocks to communication that can come from the many differences between individuals such as: authority and power; language; ability and disability; personality; background; gender; health; age; race; and class.

CASE STUDY

Sylvia, a social worker in a child protection team, visited Anne, a mother of two children, Laura (9) and David (6). Unknown to Anne, the father of one of her school friends had sexually abused Laura over a period of time. When what had been happening came to light, Anne blamed herself for not protecting Laura. Anne had also found David's behaviour challenging at times but seemed to be responding to him reasonably well. The perpetrator of the abuse, who had also sexually abused his own daughter, had left the town and was being dealt with by social workers and police a considerable distance away. At this stage, Sylvia made an assessment that there was officially no need for further action, as there was no risk of ongoing abuse. However, in listening empathetically to Anne, Sylvia realised that although the abuse had stopped, the pain and anger was not over. Her local authority's criteria threshold prevented Sylvia from offering to continue visiting to support Anne and her family. She was able, with Anne's consent, to refer her to a local voluntary organisation that offered individual and group counselling and support.

The second of Rogers' qualities is **unconditional positive regard**. Accepting the shared humanity between you and the service user is central to this. In such an atmosphere trust and partnership can develop even when a social work assessment at times includes exploring difficult areas and the service user may feel vulnerable and disempowered. Rogers also called this quality non-possessive warmth. This quality involves respect and accepting another person unconditionally, whatever they have done or are going through. In close intimate relationships this quality would equate to the unconditional love that partners or parents and children ideally have for each other.

The third quality is **self-congruence** – genuineness or 'realness'. It involves being aware of all that is going on inside yourself and being open to your own experiences. It is a feeling of integration experienced when your perception of yourself matches, or is not too far from, your ideal self – the person you aspire to be. As a social work student you may at times wonder whether you will be able to reach your own expectations of a professional worker and demonstrate the standards required of a qualified practitioner. This is something that social workers can experience throughout their careers. Genuineness can lead you to be honest about some of the complexities involved in assessment and to explain to the service user why something might or might not be possible.

Gathering information through questioning

ACTIVITY **2.2**

Talk to a friend, colleague or relative and try to hold a conversation without asking any questions. This can be based on any topic and include how you are, what you have been doing and any plans for days to come.

Comment

Did you find this activity difficult? What strategies did you use to initiate and keep communication flowing? You will no doubt have found that it is virtually impossible to communicate with another person without asking questions.

Questions are essential for assessment. They start an interview, can help pace the interaction, they elaborate and enrich what the person is telling you and can elicit concrete, factual information. As a social worker undertaking an assessment you will generally ask more questions than the service user, and the questions you ask and how you ask them can encourage or discourage discussion.

It is helpful to start interaction with open questions to allow the service user to explore their concerns. Open questions encourage service users to talk freely and openly and tend to elicit longer answers; they cannot be answered in a few short words. Closed questions can be answered with a single word or a brief sentence, typically with a 'yes' or 'no' or with short factual information. Asking the open question 'How was your journey?' is better for drawing out information from a person than the closed 'Did you have a good journey?'

The first word of an open question can lead to certain results:

- 'What' questions tend to elicit facts, e.g. 'What happened then?'

- 'How' questions explore feelings and processes and are people-oriented, e.g. 'How would you explain that?', 'How do you feel about that?'

- 'Why' questions tend to produce reasons. They can provoke defensiveness in the service user and a sense of being 'grilled' so should be used carefully and sparingly.

Questions should be clear and to the point. Multiple questions can confuse a service user.

ACTIVITY *2.3*

Paula and Denise

Below are alternative starts to their interaction.

Compare the effectiveness of closed and open questions and their use in controlling the conversation.

How might Paula feel answering questions in Start 1, compared with Start 2?

Start 1:

D: Hello, I'm Denise, a social worker on duty today. What is your name?

P: Paula.

D: Paula...? Can I have your surname?

P: Paula Covacevich.

D: That's an unusual surname, how do you spell it?

P: C O V A C E V I C H

D: Right. Is that Mrs Covacevich? Are you married?

P: I'm separated.

P: Covacevich...What nationality was your husband?

D: British, from a Croatian family.

D: Oh, interesting...So what did you want to see me about?

P: I've been finding it difficult to cope with the children...

D: Why is that? How many children do you have?

P: Two, Sam and Kelly.

D: What are their ages?

P: Sam is seven and Kelly four.

D: So are you finding it difficult to cope with both of them, or one more than the other?

Start 2:

D: Hello, I'm Denise and I'm on duty today. The receptionist told me you're Paula. Is it OK with you if I call you Paula?

P: Yes, that's fine.

D: Can you tell me why you wanted to see a social worker today?

P: Well...It's about the children...

D: (Nods head) Right...

P: I've been finding it difficult to cope with them...

D: Difficult?

P: Yes. I think Sam has been stealing money from me, and they can both be a bit of a handful.

D: OK. Can you tell me more about what is happening and how you are coping?

P: Right...Sam, he's my eldest, he's 7, is not doing very well at school and some welfare woman from the school contacted me to say he's been fighting and swearing. He's been really mouthy at home recently, he can be a little bugger at times, and I've noticed money missing from my purse. Kelly, the younger one, who's 4, is easier to cope with but lately she won't do as she's told. I think she's copying Sam.

D: I see. You must find all this difficult to cope with. Can you tell me more about what led to you deciding to come to see us here?

Comment

You will probably agree that in Start 1 Denise is controlling the conversation with closed questions, asking what she wants to know. Paula is probably frustrated that she is not being allowed to explain why she decided to come for help or advice. In Start 2, through minimal encouragers, prompts and open questions, Denise enables Paula to voice her concerns.

Even if you are required to complete a referral or an assessment framework form with specific questions, it is helpful initially to ask open questions to invite the service user to tell their story or explore their narrative. In this way you are gathering information needed for specific assessment questions, not necessarily in the order on the form.

There are questions that can prompt a service user to elaborate their narrative, e.g. 'Could you tell me more about that?' or 'Given what you have said, what would be your ideal answer?' or 'How did you feel when that happened?'

Smale, et al. (1993) suggest that in an *exchange* model of assessment, service users are viewed as experts on their situation and encouraged to develop their narrative in the exchange of information. This contrasts with a *questioning* model, in which a social worker takes the lead to find out mainly factual information, and a *procedural* model involving the use of agency assessment checklists and frameworks. These models are discussed further in Chapter 3.

When undertaking an assessment you can eventually move on to ask questions for concreteness, e.g. 'Could you give me a specific example of Sam's misbehaviour?', 'What do you mean by he drives you mad?' or 'Could you tell me more about what happens before an argument?' Closed questions can provide concreteness but take away the initiative from the service user, so you should be careful when to ask them.

A useful pictorial analogy is that an assessment interview can be like a funnel (Hargie and Dickson, 2004), starting with broad open questions and moving on to elicit concrete and accurate information. In moving from such a start to obtaining specific facts, you can use other skills mentioned earlier.

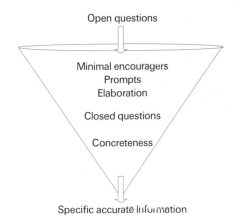

Figure 2.1

Questions worded as statements, e.g. 'It seems to me it would be helpful if you ...', can be experienced as controlling. Questioning generally can convey control. In addition to poor communication this suggests an imbalance of power. Being bombarded with questions can be a very uncomfortable experience.

RESEARCH SUMMARY

Prior to the first edition of her book, Counselling skills in social work practice (1999), Janet Seden undertook a survey of social workers using counselling skills. They were practitioners that had completed a university counselling course and were also qualified social workers working in a range of settings with varying service user groups. Respondents were asked to indicate the use in their daily practice of the skills listed. Twenty-five out of thirty responded and the results are shown in the following table. Figures are percentages of the total of returned questionnaires.

Skill	*Always*	*Percentage using skill*		
		Often	*Sometimes*	*Never*
Attention giving	71	29	0	0
Listening	93	7	0	0
Active listening	57	43	0	0
Use of empathy	28	64	8	0
Acceptance	57	28	15	0
Genuineness	28	57	15	0
Paraphrasing	30	35	35	0
Reflecting back	30	34	36	0
Summarising	38	38	24	0
Questions/exploration	20	60	20	0
Minimal prompts	21	54	25	0
Challenging	7	43	50	0
Confronting	0	56	44	0
Linking	7	50	43	0
Immediacy	7	53	40	0
Work on defences	7	40	53	0
Goal setting	28	36	36	0
Problem solving	36	64	0	0

The sample shows attending and listening skills to be the most used. It is interesting to note the frequency of skills discussed thus far in this chapter. The survey asked respondents to indicate skills used in their general social work practice, not solely assessment. The results, however, show the importance of skills that are needed in assessment although used throughout the social work process.

Communicative minorities

In a number of central and local government documents people who are not able to use traditional English verbal and non-verbal communication are described as having *special communication needs*. The term is now enshrined in legislation. Under the Mental Capacity Act (2005) a 'standard authorisation' required by care homes and hospitals to deprive someone of their liberty must include, among other requirements, whether the person has *any special communication needs*. Koprowska (2008) questions who has *special communication needs, Is it the service users, or the service providers?* Instead of labelling some people in terms of deficiencies, it is important to recognise that social workers need to develop skills and strategies to communicate with what Koprowska (p124) calls *communicative minorities*, suggesting that *as a profession we work with a very diverse group of people and we need to expand our capabilities to meet this challenge, even though we cannot be equally skilled in every area.*

As a social worker you will from time to time have to assess someone who speaks little or no English. In addition to adjustments such as speaking clearly, plainly and avoiding jargon, you will have to ensure your communication is culturally appropriate when interacting with someone from a different nationality or ethnic group. Excessive use of questions can result in someone from another culture distrusting you.

When the level of a service user's English is insufficient for assessment you may use an interpreter. This should be someone qualified and accredited, not a friend or relative as they may be emotionally involved and not able to remain objective.

Deaf persons may use British Sign Language (BSL), a language in its own right, so for them also English is not their first language. You should use a qualified and accredited interpreter rather than a possibly self-taught 'signer'. In the case of a family or when more than one deaf or hearing-impaired person is present, particularly if the assessment will last over an hour, you may need two interpreters. If working alone, the interpreter will require a break every 20 to 30 minutes. You should ask questions and interact with the person or persons being assessed, and not address the interpreter, who is there to facilitate the communication between you and the service user. Cultural awareness applies to the Deaf culture, those who are part of it regarding deafness as a difference rather than a disability. Many within the Deaf community dislike the term 'hearing impaired' as their identity is within deafness. Some reject hearing aids as an unnecessary tool to give them hearing and exclude them from the Deaf culture.

Blindness and visual impairments may result in many of the important non-verbal communication channels not being available to you. Your tone of voice is crucial in communicating helpful qualities such as openness, remaining relaxed and conveying an empathic presence. Egan's (2007) guidelines outlined earlier for *visibly tuning in* to service users will require an adjustment of skills as you are not able to achieve the tuning in visibly.

There may be some people with a physical or learning disability that impairs their speech. People with intellectual or developmental disabilities may require you to simplify your language while not being demeaning or denigrating in any way.

ACTIVITY 2.4

The following statement is adapted from information on a Council's website.

1.

Community care is about finding ways to help you to live as independently as possible. I am going to undertake a care management assessment of your needs. The level of services that may be available to assist you is determined by an assessment of your needs matched against the Council's eligibility criteria.

To start I'll have to ask you to sign a consent form to give permission for us to work with you and others that are aware of your situation, to gather information to help us develop a statement of your care needs. Once the information has been gathered, we will discuss with you what services may be available to help meet your needs. We only have a limited budget so if you don't meet our eligibility criteria we may only be able to signpost you to another service.

How would you simplify the language to give this information to someone with a learning and intellectual disability? It might be something like this:

2.

Our work is to help you to manage to do the things you want to do. I'm going to ask you questions to find out how you are managing. I then have to find out how much we can help you. We give more help to those that need it more, so we can't help everybody.

Before we start, can I ask you to sign a form to say it is OK for me to work with you and with others that know you to get information to show me how you are managing. When we have all the information we can talk about what you need and what might help you most. We only have enough money to help those that need a lot of help so I might only be able to tell you about other people you can go to.

Comment

Would you use the first statement to start an assessment with any adult service user? There is a danger of using jargon familiar to us. If the second statement was the start of your interaction with a learning disabled person you would need to check their understanding, listen carefully and allow the service user to finish what they are saying, which may take longer due to slower cognitive processes and speech.

Dementias and other forms of confusion typically affect a person's ability to think and to reason. When making an assessment of a person with a cognitive impairment, relatives are often present. It is important for you to engage and ask questions of the person being assessed rather than rely on someone else to mediate communication or give you information. Closed questions may be appropriate with someone with a learning disability or dementia. Phillips, et al. (2006, p116) suggest that open questions may cause *fear, anxiety, suspicion and embarrassment.*

In considering age-appropriate communication, as well as with older persons, there are implications for assessing children and young people. Skills involved will include adjusting language and interaction accordingly and taking into account a child's level of cognitive understanding and attention spans. It is often better to engage in an activity with a child or young person through which communication will take place in a way that may be difficult if you are relying on a formal interview setting. In assessing a child's perception of their family, for instance, it can be helpful to use buttons or toys to represent people. Drawing is also a useful way of communicating. Wilson and Powell (2001) stress the importance of preparation and planning and suggest useful techniques to tailor an interview to the child's needs.

Uncooperative service users

There will be times when as a social worker you will be dealing with people who are resistant or reluctant to engage with you. There may also be times when you have to investigate circumstances to safeguard people from neglect and abuse. This is particularly so in child protection assessments.

Egan (2007) makes a distinction between reluctance and resistance. He refers to *reluctance* to engage due to hesitancy, anxiety and fear of consequences. Some service users may be reluctant to talk about themselves and their circumstances. Egan (2007, p184) explains *resistance* as *the push back from clients when they feel they are being coerced.* This may apply to service users that think they are being mistreated or to those who believe that their cultural beliefs, values and norms are being violated. It can include involuntary service users such as offenders and, for different reasons, Black and minority ethnic service users.

Skills of active listening and communicating accurate empathy will help dissipate reluctance. Skills such as giving feedback and challenging may be involved in interacting with a service user who is resistant to the assessment. Cultural- and age-appropriate skills would also be of importance; fully involving the service user as a participant in the assessment is crucial.

CASE STUDY

Claudia, a student on placement in a Young Offenders Team, was allocated work with 15-year-old Justin on a referral order following a first but serious shoplifting offence. He seemed to cooperate when he came before a youth offender panel and accepted a six-month contract to see a worker regularly to discuss his behaviour. However, after a first rather unproductive meeting he missed two further appointments and Claudia wrote pointing out he was in breach of his order and making an appointment to visit him at home.

When she visited, Claudia found Justin very hostile. He was tall and standing rather close to Claudia, shouting that he didn't want to have any f**ing order and she could f*** off out of his house. Claudia, who was 20, so not that much older than Justin, immediately felt that her social work degree teaching about good communication skills and Rogerian qualities had not prepared her to deal with this. Although she was anxious, she remained

→

CASE STUDY continued

calm and sat down. She said she realised Justin was angry and, rather than telling him not to swear and speak to her like that, she asked him what he had been doing in the last two weeks. Using open questions, encouragers and prompts, she slowly encouraged him to talk about being unhappy at home and not doing well at school. In the first session Claudia had given Justin a self-report questionnaire to assess antisocial attitudes and offending behaviour. He was too embarrassed to tell her he did not understand it all due to his low reading age. She could empathise with his response and reactions and reflected this back to him.

Investigative interviewing

The term 'investigative' is more commonly associated with interviewing by police officers. Social workers also sometimes have to assess very difficult situations involving possible neglect or abuse. Exploring investigative interviewing, Milne and Bull (1999, p63) refer to six micro-skills originally proposed by Shepherd (1986):

1. *Observation and memory.*

2. *Listening and assertion – where appropriate listening results in assertion being seen as acceptable.*

3. *Initiating and regulating through the process of control and social reinforcement.*

4. *Appropriate questioning which allows the elicitation and subsequent probing of the initial and subsequent interviewee accounts.*

5. *Active listening and information processing.*

6. *Confronting feelings, reflecting back and summarising.*

We have already highlighted some of the skills involved, which can be applied to an investigation. Other skills are suggested that can be appropriate to social work investigations. Careful observation is crucial; you will sometimes need to pay attention to bruising and injuries and ask about them. You may have to ask to see a child when parents say he or she is fine and sleeping, out or not available. You may have to ask to see bedrooms and other rooms, and observe whether anything in them, or the absence of essential items, may suggest the risk of significant harm or neglect.

You will be expected to remember inconsistencies in service users' accounts and challenge them. You should take the initiative to ask about what may be difficult and sensitive areas. Assertiveness skills are appropriate in such circumstances. Assertiveness is the centre of a continuum where at one end you are behaving passively, not initiating purposeful interaction, and at the other end you are demanding information in an aggressive way.

Hargie and Dickson (2004, p309) suggest that *in order to execute assertiveness skills effectively, three central components need to be mastered: content, process and nonverbal responses.* Assertive content should be clear and to the point, honest and open, without the 'padding' of an apologetic approach, unnecessary explanations or elaborate complexity.

The process that goes on between people interacting with each other is important. You should not get involved in double meanings or underlying assumptions. At appropriate times you may point out that you need to ask the professional opinion of another person or simply ask for time to think when you feel pressured.

Hargie and Dickson (2004, p312) state that non-verbal responses involve

> *medium levels of eye contact; avoidance of inappropriate facial expression; smooth use of gestures while speaking, yet inconspicuous while listening; upright posture; direct body orientation; medium interpersonal distance; and appropriate paralinguistics (short response latency, medium response length, good fluency, medium volume and inflection, increased firmness).*

Milne and Bull (1999, p63) go on to say that it is only when you have reached acceptable levels in the six micro-skills listed above that you can reach a higher four macro-skills level:

1. *The ability to detect changes in interviewee non-verbal behaviour across the interview which some believe to indicate evasion/deception.*

2. *The ability to detect changes in emotional state, motivation, attitude and disposition.*

3. *The ability to build a global picture of the interview as a whole – a macro-structure.*

4. *The ability to identify indicators and patterns of vagueness, ambiguity and contradiction by evaluating the interviewee's account.*

While your approach as a social worker will clearly not be initially to expect evasion, deception and contradictions, you will come across these responses.

CASE STUDY

The Haringey Local Safeguarding Children Board's Serious Case Review of 'Child A' (2008), a 17-month-old boy later identified as baby Peter Connelly following his tragic death and national publicity, states that his mother was considered to be cooperating with the child protection plans. The apparently positive observations of the mother's parenting led to a high level of trust of her. New incidents were interpreted in terms of the existing understandings of the family dynamics, with insufficient attempts to use the incidents to prompt reassessments. Sadly, professionals failed to discern information such as the fact that a Mr H who had a close relationship with the child's mother was living within the household and that for some two weeks before the baby's death a friend of Mr H, Mr G, his three children and a 15-year-old female whom he described as his girlfriend had been staying there. Signs casting doubts on the child's health and well-being were missed. The baby's mother, Mr H and Mr G went on to be charged with murder and causing or allowing the death of a child.

Analysing and recording information

When assessing you will be gathering information, organising and evaluating it, deciding how much of it is relevant and accurate, comparing and contrasting information gathered from different sources. Critical thinking, analysis and evaluation are necessary to achieve these tasks. In summarising what is involved to develop as a critical practitioner, Jones (2009, p121) comes to the conclusion that it means

> *analysing what has happened, how it happened and why; what our responses might be and why the one we choose appears at that time to be the best possible response. In addition you should be considering what might be the possible outcomes of action that you chose not to take.*

Social workers are sometimes accused of gathering information but then not having the skills to analyse it and make professional judgements. In writing about *Forming decisions and making judgements*, Trevithick (2005, p61) states that

> *it is important to highlight the importance of being able to form independent, balanced, courageous and sometimes critical judgements, based on critical thinking and the 'best evidence' available to us at the time.*

Skills involved in assessment include recording information correctly. You will need to keep accurate records of information and conclusions. The service user has a right see a copy of everything you have written and agree with it. You should inform service users how to access their files and make complaints if they are not satisfied.

An interesting development is the use of laptops to record information. In their online information about *Who does what in adult social care services*, Wolverhampton City Council, for instance, state that a *service information officer will often be the first person a customer will discuss their problem with.* The use of the term 'customer' in itself suggests a buyer or purchaser of products or services. The website goes on to say that *when a customer's circumstances are complex, the case may be transferred to a social work assessment team to deal with.* An assessor will visit *and complete complex, multidisciplinary assessments, using mobile technology such as laptops, if necessary.*

While there may be advantages in the use of technology, such as access to information and efficient use of time, there is a danger that important interpersonal communication skills may suffer. Even if not using laptops, you will be required to take notes and complete appropriate documentation when undertaking an assessment. It is best not to start noting information down immediately, but to ask the service user to tell you about themselves in the funnel approach outlined earlier. When moving on to concreteness and the gathering of specific information, it will be necessary for you to note it down accurately.

A challenge then is to indicate involvement, be open, lean slightly towards the person being assessed, maintain appropriate eye contact, show attention and listen actively while also noting information by writing it down or entering it onto a laptop.

C H A P T E R   S U M M A R Y

This chapter encouraged you to consider interpersonal communication skills needed to undertake social work assessments. It suggested that at one level they are simple, as you have used many of them throughout your life. However, the chapter also highlighted the complexity of communication between human beings with individual experiences and perceptions about themselves and their circumstances.

The chapter reviewed skills involved in hearing, attending, non-verbal communication, active listening, reflecting, paraphrasing and summarising. It also introduced you to the personal qualities of empathy, unconditional positive regard and congruence, recognising that skills are needed to demonstrate these qualities to service users.

The chapter encouraged you to become more aware of the importance of questions in social work assessments and introduced you to different types of questions such as open, closed, prompts and elaborative ones. It suggested a *funnel sequence* for social work assessments, starting with open questions and moving with the use of minimal encouragers through prompts and elaboration to ask closed questions to obtain concrete and accurate information.

We considered how to put skills into practice with *communicative minorities* such as communicating with people for whom English is not their first language, including BSL, the use of interpreters, and communicating with people with other impairments, dementias and confusion.

Through consideration of the reluctance and resistance that you may encounter in some service users, the chapter introduced you to skills involved in investigative interviewing.

Finally, the chapter reminded you of the importance of analysing and evaluating information critically and recording it accurately.

FURTHER READING

Egan, G (2007) *The skilled helper: A problem-management and opportunity development approach to helping*. 8th edition. London: Thomson Learning.
As the subtitle suggests, this textbook presents a comprehensive practice model for helping professionals. Chapters 4 to 9 in Part 2: The therapeutic dialogue, outline skills relevant to assessment.

Hargie, O and Dickson, D (2004) *Skilled interpersonal communication: Research, theory and practice.* Hove: Routledge.
Although not written specifically for social work, this textbook thoroughly explores communication skills backed with research evidence. It devotes chapters to important areas such as, among others, non-verbal communication, questioning, reflecting, listening and assertiveness.

Koprowska, J (2010) *Communication and interpersonal skills in social work.* 3rd edition. Exeter: Learning Matters Ltd.
In addition to exploring effective communication generally, this textbook has chapters devoted to communicating with children, families and groups and *communicative minorities*.

Seden, J (2005) *Counselling skills in social work practice*. 2nd edition. Maidenhead: Open University Press.
The writer helpfully reviews counselling and interpersonal communication skills used in social work, including Chapter 3 Assessment: relevant counselling skills.

Chapter 3
Theoretical underpinning to assessment

Problem-solving skills.

5.5.3 Analysis and synthesis.

- Assess human situations, taking into account a variety of factors (including the views of participants, theoretical concepts, research evidence, legislation and organisational policies and procedures).
- Assess the merits of contrasting theories, explanations, research, policies and procedures.

Introduction

This chapter will explore ways in which theory informs the practice of undertaking social work assessments. That is not to say that all other chapters do not review theoretical ideas; however, the specific focus of this chapter is on the integration of underpinning theory with practice.

> **REFLECTION POINT**
>
> *Do you think there is a need for social work practitioners to have theoretical knowledge? How confident do you feel about your ability to be guided by theory in your practice? What theories do you think might be useful in assessment?*

Comment

If you did not answer *yes* to the first question you may not be looking forward to this chapter, in fact you may struggle with the whole notion of a textbook about social work assessment! If your feelings are ambivalent or suggest some uncertainty and anxiety when reflecting on your confidence about theory, you are not alone. Many students and practitioners say they find theory 'scary' or 'off-putting'. Many wonder 'What theory shall I use?'

When students start learning theoretical ideas on a social work programme and are faced with a case study or an actual referral on a practice placement they may immediately wonder what theory to use, doing so almost as if they need to fit the information into a theoretical straitjacket. It feels more like fitting practice into theory rather than how underpinning theory, or theories, might inform and facilitate practice.

As part of the above reflection you may even have wondered, 'What do we mean by theory?' In exploring the role of theory Payne, (2005, p5) questions *how do social workers know what to do when they do social work?* He proposes that *a theory is an organised statement of ideas about the world,* and suggests that:

> *In social work, the term 'theory' covers three different possibilities:*
>
> - *Models that provide principles and patterns to structure and organise practice. A good example is task-centred practice ...*
> - *Perspectives providing values or views of the world. Examples of perspectives are feminist ... or systems theories ...*

- *Explanatory theories offering causal explanations. Cognitive-behavioural theory ... is an example.*

A difficulty is that different writers use terms in different ways, so what we mean by 'theory' can be open to debate. Some use the term 'grand theories' to refer to what Payne (2005) calls *perspectives*. These are broad, overarching ideas such as Marxism and feminism.

There are what some writers call 'standard theories' or disciplines, such as psychology, sociology and social policy. Within these there are particular approaches that some may call perspectives. In social work, theoretical ideas inform practice methods and models. As a social worker you may be informed by theory to support a service user through a crisis, challenge their cognitive behavioural patterns, work on tasks to achieve agreed goals, or a combination of these. Theoretical thinking will influence your assessment. Coulshed and Orme (2006) argue that *there is no such thing as 'theoryless' practice*, so it follows that there is no such thing as 'theoryless' assessment.

In a review of social work assessment textbooks and frameworks Crisp, et al. (2005) conclude that there is no single theory for assessment. They found a variety of theoretical underpinning to assessment including:

- from psychology and social psychology: behavioural theory, psychodynamic approaches and solution-focused and task-focused perspectives;

- varieties of post-modern perspectives, including narrative and discourse analysis and critical constructionism;

- models based on systems theory and social exchange theory.

Using these three broad categories, we will now move on to review a variety of theoretical ideas.

From psychology and social psychology
Psychodynamic approaches

Drawing on the original theorising of Sigmund Freud (1856–1939), psychodynamic approaches suggest that our behaviour can be explained in terms of inner motives developed in early childhood.

Freud's early conceptualising led to a 'topographical' model of mental life. The conscious level, like the exposed part of an iceberg, is our awareness of thoughts and perceptions. Just below the surface of awareness is the pre-conscious level – our memories and stored knowledge, which may give clues about unconscious forces that determine our actions. The largest, submerged part of the 'iceberg' is the unconscious level – our secret, irrational wishes and fears, sexual desires, violent motives and selfish wants.

These ideas developed into a psychodynamic 'structural' model of personality.

- The *Id* is our mainly unconscious source of sexual and aggressive instinctual drives and biological urges seeking immediate gratification and wish-fulfilment.

- Opposing the demands of the id is the *Superego*, the moral and judicial part of our personality made up of internalised values and moral imperatives. It includes general social and cultural restrictions, and learned concepts about right and wrong.

- Mediating between the id and superego is the *Ego,* a realistic and logical, 'executive' part of our personality. It tests reality before acting and accepts delayed gratification.

There is moral conflict between the ego and superego and neurotic conflict between the ego and the id. In addition, our inner personality structure has to cope with external reality and conflict. This creates a psychodynamic mixture of internal and external conflict that may lead to dreams, neurotic symptoms and defence mechanisms.

Defence mechanisms are ego coping strategies when faced with the anxiety produced by unconscious conflict. They involve an element of self-deceit and include *denial* of unpleasant or threatening realities, *repression* of traumatic memories, *rationalisation* of unacceptable motives, *projection* of unwanted thoughts and feelings onto external factors and *displacement* of anxiety-provoking instinctual wishes onto more acceptable objects or people.

When undertaking an assessment you may be asking a service user about their awareness of thoughts and feelings. They may recount memories that seem to be below the surface until you explore aspects of their lives with them. Psychoanalytic theory may suggest assessing an individual's ego strength and defence mechanisms. This can aid the work of supporting people during crisis intervention.

CASE STUDY

Adelle and Mavis

Adelle was undertaking a care management assessment of 83-year-old Mavis to ascertain the extent to which she could cope practically at home. Adelle found Mavis a difficult person, with apparently self-centred and selfish views. Adelle took a few minutes from completing assessment forms to ask Mavis about her background and life. Mavis shared memories of her husband who died some years earlier. Adelle understood Mavis as someone with unconscious processes affecting her behaviour. Not only was she displaying defence mechanisms such as repression to deal with the death of her husband, but the experience made Mavis transfer feelings to others and regress to a time when her own parents died many years before.

Adelle was aware of the psychodynamic concept of transference when a service user transfers to the social worker unconscious feelings and wishes. She was also careful about counter-transference when the social worker may have negative or positive feelings towards the service user.

Attachment theory

Schaffer and Emerson (1964) described attachment as *a close emotional relationship between two persons, characterised by mutual affection and a desire to maintain proximity (closeness).* John Bowlby (1907–1990), a key attachment theorist initially influenced by the British School of Psychoanalysis, suggested that an infant's attachment to their mother, or care-giver, influences their subsequent interactions and relationships for the rest of their life. The child seeks an 'attachment figure' for safety and protection and to act as a secure base from which to explore the environment. He suggested the child has an innate need for an attachment figure (monotropy). Bowlby's *maternal deprivation hypothesis* suggests that a failure to make, or a breakdown of, the maternal attachment will lead to serious negative consequences.

Other theorists widened Bowlby's approach, showing through research that children could form more than one attachment and that some could be mainly attached to their father. Rutter (1981) suggested that there was a difference between *deprivation* through being separated after forming an attachment, and *privation* through never having formed a close attachment.

Children develop 'internal working models' – internalised representations or schemata – which for secure attachment would include 'My parents are there for me', 'They care for me', 'I can trust them'.

As a social worker you may assess factors contributing to the forming of secure attachment, such as a positive pre-natal period and pregnancy, secure adult attachment in the parents and early bonding at birth. The first six months are important in terms of parent–child interaction and exchanges, including body contact. Infants tend to develop a strong attachment to one person around 7 to 8 months and display fear and anxiety of strangers around 6 to 12 months.

Through filming 'strange situations', Ainsworth, et al. (1978) studied how children coped with the stress of being left alone by their care-givers with a stranger for short periods and observed *secure*, *avoidant* or *anxious/ambivalent* attachment patterns. A fourth *disorganised* category was identified by Main and Solomon (1986), and some writers such as Howe (1995) have suggested a pattern of *non attachment*. Disorganised attachment is a set of precise behaviours only visible under certain conditions that activate the attachment system, suggesting the child has no clear strategy for responding to care-givers. These may include avoiding or resisting the care-giver, being confused or frightened by them, and occasionally freezing or being still when a care-giver approaches. The behaviours are only temporary, after which the child reverts to one of the three organised attachment patterns.

The internal working model for avoidant attachment might include, 'I can't rely on my parents', 'I can't depend on them', ' I will look after myself'; and for ambivalent attachment, 'I am not worth bothering about', 'I want my parents to be there for me but they are bound to let me down', 'I am desperate for their care'.

RESEARCH SUMMARY

Empson and Nabuzoka (2004) review theoretical approaches to atypical child development situations such as child abuse, emotional and behavioural difficulties and learning disabilities. They summarise characteristics of different patterns of attachment.

Attachment pattern	Characteristics of self	Characteristics of others	Frequency in population
Secure	Loved, effective, autonomous, competent	Available, cooperative, dependable	55%
Avoidant	Unloved but self-reliant	Rejecting, intrusive	23%
Ambivalent	Low value, ineffective, dependent	Neglecting, insensitive, unpredictable	8%
Insecure-disorganised	Confused, bad	Frightening, unavailable	15%

The percentages for the frequency of attachment patterns in the population are from van Ijzendoorm, et al. (1992), a meta-analysis reviewing 34 clinical studies. Their results show that for groups where maternal problems have been identified, attachment classification distributions are highly divergent from the normal distributions, whereas groups where child problems have been identified show distributions that are similar to the distributions of normal samples. Thus the mother's sensitivity appears to play a more important role than the child in shaping the quality of the infant–mother attachment relationship.

Theories of attachment are important beyond work with children and families. In adolescence, parents tend to remain as attachment figures while the young person goes through a transition into adulthood and attachment behaviour usually becomes increasingly directed towards peers. Theorists have suggested that a person's early attachment relation with parents influences subsequent relationships in adult life. Attachment scales have been designed to test adult attachment. Versions of these are used by fostering and adoption social workers to assess prospective carers and parents.

Cognitive development

Unlike animals, as human beings we develop cognitive abilities including logical thinking, language and problem solving.

The development of cognitive processes is a way for humans to adapt to their environment through constructing an understanding of reality by interacting with it. Knowledge does not come 'ready-made', it has to be actively discovered, whether it is an infant fitting plastic pieces in a shape-sorter toy or you trying to make sense of theoretical ideas in this chapter.

Piaget (1896–1980) proposed infants had to develop schemata – internal assumptions or units of cognitive understanding. Sucking may be an example of an early instinctual schema used to explore objects. More advanced schemata may be concepts, such as 'mummy', 'daddy' and learning that not all women are 'mummy' nor all men 'daddy'.

Piaget suggested that the process of adapting to the environment involves:

- *assimilation* of what is perceived in the outside world by incorporating it internally and fitting it into existing schemata;
- *accommodation* of the internal world to external evidence and adapting to it, thus developing new schemata.

He put forward four stages of cognitive development.

Sensori-motor stage from birth to approximately 18 months or 2 years. Infants learn to interpret information through the five senses and are also learning muscle, or motor, coordination, grasping objects, as a way of interacting with the environment.

Pre-operational stage from approximately 2 to 6 or 7 years. Children learn to use language and gradually discover rules such as conservation – realising there is the same amount of clay when a ball of it is rolled into a different shape, liquid is poured into a different-shaped container or buttons spread over a wider area. These 'operations' are concepts or schemata, so this could be termed a pre-conceptual stage when children have a mainly 'egocentric' outlook and find it difficult to perceive things from someone else's point of view.

Concrete-operational stage from approximately 7 to 11 or 12 years. Children begin to work things out mentally and understand concepts. They can solve problems by thinking about them, rather than having to play with models, but may not yet be able to deal with abstract concepts or operations.

Formal operational stage from approximately 12 years to adulthood. Young people learn to reason logically in a way that they should be able to do throughout life.

There are theorists who took Piaget's ideas further. Some suggested there are more than four stages and put forward 'problem finding', 'post-formal' or dialectical thinking stages. The Russian psychologist Lev Vygotsky (1896–934) highlighted social and cultural factors by suggesting that children's knowledge, values and attitudes develop through social interaction.

A children and families social worker can benefit from knowledge about cognitive development when assessing a family. It will be important to be aware of a child's level of cognitive understanding when parents discipline them or when a social worker explains reasons for an assessment and possible outcomes. A child who is not at a stage to perceive things from someone else's point of view may construe abuse as their fault. Their logic will be that if they are abused it must be because they are bad or unlovable, not because an abusive adult is doing something wrong.

Behavioural approach and learning theory

To explain any behaviour we can consider how we learn to behave as we do. A behavioural approach suggests learning through life is a process of conditioning.

Classical conditioning is learning by forming new associations, as dogs did when Pavlov (1849–1936) conditioned them to salivate through the association between the sound of a bell and food. Classical conditioning may explain fears and phobias. Fear of dogs may be the result of a previous, perhaps forgotten, frightening incident with a dog. A panic reaction to open or crowded spaces could be the result of an earlier anxiety-provoking experience.

Operant conditioning involves learning through the consequences of behaviour. Skinner (1904–90) conditioned rats to press a lever that produced a pellet of food. He was able to 'shape' the behaviour of pigeons by increasingly rewarding steps towards behaviour such as turning around. Applying this to humans, the praise of parents is a powerful reward for children and many teachers and parents use rewards, which may be sweets, a star chart or earning privileges such as pocket money.

Behavioural theory suggests the environment must be changed, not the 'inner self', to achieve a change in behaviour. A social worker assessing a family where the parents are finding it difficult to manage a child's behaviour may use an ABC (Antecedents – Behaviour – Consequences) sequence to help parents understand the principles.

CASE STUDY

Susan, a family support social worker, is assessing a family where parents, Paul and June, are finding it difficult to manage the behaviour of their middle child Ben (10). Paul and June say Ben is 'difficult', 'disobedient', 'aggressive' and has 'temper tantrums'. Explaining the ABC sequence and starting with B for behaviour, Susan asks about Ben's specific difficult behaviour. What does he do and when? Paul and June say he shouts at them, cries and swears. His aggression results in kicking, biting, scratching and hitting his parents and siblings. It is a struggle to get Ben to bed and he does not stay in it when they take him. Turning to A for antecedents, Susan explores what happens before Ben behaves as they describe. What seems to trigger it? They give an example when Paul told Ben to stop watching TV and go to bed after June had said he could watch a few more minutes. This resulted in an argument between Paul and June. Using C for consequences, Susan asks what happens after Ben misbehaves. They say they often resort to shouting back and smacking him and that he joins in their arguments. Susan explains it would be much better for them to ignore Ben's misbehaviour as much as possible and reward him when he behaves well. Before further discussion of strategies to take Ben to bed, and keep him there, and a reward system that Ben can understand, Susan asks Paul and June to keep a diary of Ben's ABC sequence for a week until she comes to see them again.

Humanistic insights

Carl Rogers (1902–87) and Abraham Maslow (1908–70) were critical of a psycho-analytic approach where behaviour is determined by inner conflicts, and of the similar deterministic and mechanistic conditioning explanations of behaviourists. They proposed a 'third force' in psychology, suggesting our subjective experiences are as valid a field of study as the clinical deductions of psychoanalysts and the scientific measurement of behaviourists.

This approach proposes that human beings are largely free to shape themselves and determine their own destinies – to grow and develop. Healthy development is a natural tendency in humans. Life's essential motive is to 'self-actualise', leading to being a fully functioning person.

Humanistic theorists accepted that individuals are also influenced by environmental variables. Unemployment, poor education and living standards, and conditional acceptance from others such as our parents, are not conditions conducive to growth.

To illustrate what motivates human beings towards self-actualisation, Maslow put forward a hierarchy of needs that have to be met sequentially and cumulatively. They are represented in a well-known triangle or pyramid with the most basic needs forming the base, building up to the peak of self-actualisation. Working from the most basic upwards, the needs are:

- physiological – including food, water, warmth, shelter, sleep, excretion;

- safety – such as physical safety and order but also a sense of psychological safety;

- belonging and love – family and other meaningful groups, friendships, intimate relationships;

- esteem – self-esteem leading to confidence and achievement and stemming from having the esteem of others through their respect and recognition;

- self-actualisation – a mature approach to life, problem solving, understanding moral issues, creativity, spontaneity and lack of prejudice, all leading to self-fulfilment.

CASE STUDY

Adelle and Mavis

Having understood Mavis much better, Adelle assessed that she was isolated, as many of her peers had died and she had few friends. She had a poor self-image and low self-esteem. However, Adelle first had to discuss with Mavis and help her with physiological needs as she was not eating well or taking physical care of herself and she did not feel safe physically or psychologically. A care package of delivered meals and personal carers had to address these needs before Adelle could suggest and Mavis agree to attendance at a day centre.

Rogers (1961) highlighted the importance of relating to each other to achieve conditions for growth. He proposed that we need:

- accurate empathy – the ability to understand someone else's subjective experience is at the heart of a humanistic understanding of fellow humans;

- unconditional positive regard – the acceptance and caring given to a fellow human, without imposing conditions on how the person behaves, is crucial to meet the needs for belonging, love and esteem;

- self-congruence – a genuineness or 'realness' experienced as an integration of our self-concept and the person we aspire to be is essential for self-actualisation.

We came across these personal qualities in Chapter 2 as fundamental to a person-centred approach in being 'helpful' to others. We can now see them as integral to the philosophical underpinning of this theoretical perspective.

Social learning

Different theoretical approaches can clash or be contradictory but can also be complementary. Accepting human subjective experience as playing a part in social work assessment reminds us that thoughts, feelings, expectations and values are important in how we behave. We have now seen how cognitive processes mediate between the environment and behaviour. So the question of how we are socialised into our culture can be explained as a social cognitive or cognitive behavioural perspective.

From the 1950s Albert Bandura undertook research studies into social learning and aggression, some involving groups of children watching a film of an adult being aggressive to a large plastic 'bobo' doll. In one film version the adult 'role model' was rewarded at the end with compliments, sweets and lemonade. In another the adult was scolded and warned not to be aggressive. When the children were put in the same situation they imitated the aggressive behaviour. A group of children that saw negative consequences initially showed significantly less aggression. However, when asked to imitate the aggression, they did so. The difference for this group seemed to be one of behavioural performance or imitation, not of cognitive learning or acquisition. This seems to point towards a difference between 'knowing' and 'doing'.

As a social worker undertaking an assessment, you may find a theoretical understanding of vicarious learning of new behaviour in social situations useful. This may explain adolescent experimentation in groups. Children's behaviour related to fear or confidence may have been learned through watching the emotional reactions of others. Adults may use problem-solving strategies learned from others dealing with challenges. Role models are very influential in society.

Social learning theory suggests that social and moral behaviour are acquired in the same way. Classical conditioning can explain our conscience as a conditioned emotional response. Being disciplined results in associating anxiety with punishment. Operant conditioning can explain how the behaviour we engage in voluntarily is conditioned by rewards and punishments.

Cognitive behavioural approach

Informed by behavioural and social learning theories and knowledge of cognitive development, social workers can enable service users to prioritise and work on issues in their lives. Macdonald (2007, p169) points out that *once people have acquired an ability to think cognitive-behaviourally, they become more adept at analysing and intervening in problematic situations, without recourse to professional intervention.*

Aaron Beck (1976) and Albert Ellis (1979) emphasised the importance of cognition in psychotherapy. They suggested faulty cognitions and ways of thinking and flawed reasoning are important factors in depression and other mental health conditions. Beck used three key concepts to explain depression:

1. A negative 'cognitive triad' way of individuals regarding themselves, their current situations and their prospects. In a 'negative cognitive shift' individuals ignore any positive information and only accept or perceive negative aspects about themselves.

2. Schemata involved in looking at the world – assimilating previous experience into negative schemata and an inability to adapt thinking in more positive ways.

3. Faulty information processing and flawed reasoning that arise from biased schemata.

CASE STUDY

Irene, a social worker from a Community Mental Health Team, is using a cognitive behavioural approach to assess Haley, a 34-year-old service user who psychiatrists have diagnosed as suffering from depression and anxiety. Using open questions, Irene explores Haley's expectations. Together they prioritise problems that Haley wants to work on, including low self-esteem, looking for work and attending interviews, which Haley finds difficult unless a friend accompanies her. Irene assesses Haley's behaviour and expectations, including her thoughts, feelings and values. She plans to teach Haley cognitive principles such as her rewarding and punishing reactions, disputing and challenging faulty cognitive assumptions about herself and encourage Haley to continue the work on her own.

Task-centred perspective

This is not so much a theory underpinning assessment but a mode of practice that has come from within social work itself rather than being adapted from another discipline. It was quite radical in the 1960s to propose that a social worker might negotiate with the service user a programme of help and come to an agreement about the problems to be addressed and how goals would be achieved within a short-term period of time. The model arose from research by William Reid examining the influence of training and experience on workers' responses, leading to a study published by Reid and Shyne (1969) comparing *brief and extended casework.*

In assessment you would initially examine problems by considering all the areas that might need help. This can be wide ranging without at this stage concentrating on any particular problems in depth. You can then analyse and discuss problems in more detail, prioritising them and taking the service user's views into account, unless there are statutory considerations that the service user needs to address.

Your assessment would include negotiating time limits for the duration of the work. If there is a reason for longer-term involvement, you can negotiate a series of steps involving shorter-term agreements, involving the service user in the process.

This way of working clearly demonstrates the social work process. Assessment entails a joint exploration of problems with the service user. Planning involves outlining the goals to be achieved. Intervention then proceeds in a series of incremental steps, as you and the service user engage in a number of tasks to work towards achieving the agreed goals. This is subject to regular review.

Solution-focused approach

Another mode of practice, more than a theory underpinning assessment, is solution-focused brief therapy, which originated in the mid-1980s within psychotherapy and counselling disciplines. de Shazer (1985) proposed that, however serious or fixed the problems, there are always exceptions that can contain the seeds of the service user's own solution. Thus solution building rather than problem solving became the focus. In three to eight sessions at most, a worker explores a person's resources and future hopes rather than current problems and past causes.

As a social worker using this approach, you would be interested to determine with the service user the goals of intervention so that you would know when it was time to end. The clearer a service user is about their goals the more likely it is that the goals will be achieved. Rather than the more traditional information gathering and analysis assessment focus, finding ways to identify and describe future goals are central to solution-focused brief work. Instead of discussing problems, your attention would be focused on developing a picture of the solution and discovering resources to achieve it. You might ask what has become known as the 'miracle' question. If overnight a miracle happened and it resolved the problems you want to tackle, what would you notice that was different tomorrow? Your assessment would involve finding out:

- what the person is hoping to achieve through a brief period of contact with a social worker; exploration of a preferred future perhaps based on the miracle question;

- what the small, everyday details of the person's life would be if these hopes were realised; the changes that the person would notice if suddenly problems were resolved;

- what the person is already doing or has been able to do in the past that might contribute to these goals being achieved. Coping strategies already used, including perseverance, not giving up hope, history of past successes and achievements;

- what might be different if the person made one very small step towards achieving the goals; things others would notice if the person made that small step.

Your focus would be on what the service user is already doing that might help achieve a solution. The emphasis on the preferred future makes the service user's view of the problem redundant. The service user needs to want something different, even if at first they do not think that it is possible. Sometimes service users' lives are so difficult that they cannot imagine things being different and are very negative about their present circumstances. You can ask how they cope and manage to continue in spite of adversity.

Varieties of post-modern perspectives, including narrative and discourse analysis and critical constructionism

In a review of 'modern' and 'post-modern' ideas, Payne (2005) points out that in the 1700s and 1800s *we relied on the authority of religion and monarchs to tell us how to think.* The 'modern' approach that followed was the acceptance that we could develop knowledge by observing and experimenting with the real world through *scientific* methods. Payne argues that social work is a product of *modernism* as one of the secular replacements for the welfare role of the Christian churches in Western countries. He continues:

> It is also modernist because it is based on the idea that we can understand and study social problems and societies, and take rational action to deal with problems per se.

(Payne, 2005, p15)

Most of the theoretical ideas outlined thus far in this chapter had the underlying assumption that in social work assessment you can gather information to understand the problems of service users and plan action to deal with them.

Post-modernism suggests that there are alternative ways to think about knowledge and understanding. It points out that knowledge is always socially constructed. Your choosing to ask about and observe particular aspects of a service user's world will be based on your training, theoretical understanding and experience. If you are assessing a child's developmental needs, parenting capacity and family and environmental factors, your assessment will be based on your 'constructed' ideas of typical child development and what a family is. The language you use will be a vehicle for inherent assumptions.

Post-modernism challenges any social knowledge, suggesting you cannot understand reality without understanding historical and social contexts.

Parton and O'Byrne (2000) point out that *the notion of assessment sits uncomfortably in the constructionist frame.* They put forward a new practice perspective of constructive social work. It is constructive because it builds on the positives in people's lives and experiences and uses ideas drawn from social construction theory. There are links between social constructionism and a brief solution-focused approach.

A starting point is people's *narratives* as they describe events to try to make their story correspond to reality as they perceive it. Their narrative is their reality. That representation of reality also takes into account the narrator's perception of the people listening. Hence a narrative emerges from and interacts with events. An analysis of a service user's narrative or discourse requires sensitive listening and getting inside their story, including images and metaphors used to describe a problem.

CASE STUDY

Ennis is care manager for Megan, a 25-year-old woman with severe learning difficulties. He has made an assessment of Megan's needs and has been in contact with the family for some months, but today he is visiting June, Megan's mother, to discuss her needs as a carer.

At first June suggests she copes well, but through gentle encouragement and sensitive listening from Ennis, she expands. She says she can get tired and worn out, as if her 'batteries are low'. There can be arguments at home, although 'it's nobody's fault'. At one point June talks impersonally about carers, saying mostly they 'just get on with it'. People should realise that there is not 'just a disabled person', not 'just a carer', but 'the whole family is under the strain'. June says 'all of us' tend to have two faces – 'the public face' that includes 'laughing and full of fun' and the 'behind the front door face' when 'people don't know what they are going to find when they get home, what will happen next, whether the family will be in a good or bad mood'. She says 'you feel like you are in a box with a label – if this is what your child is, this is what you are'.

In an exchange of responses, Ennis resists the temptation to immediately suggest solutions. Although June referred to carers in general and about issues people should be aware of, Ennis understands she is talking about herself and asks if she feels she 'just has to get on with caring' and whether there are different things she would like to do at times. Using some of her images, he asks whether going past the front door into the house ever feels like going into a labelled box and what is the label?

June acknowledges that some of Ennis's help for Megan has felt like 'a big weight lifted off' her shoulders. She says about herself, 'I am me, not a carer, not a mum, I am an individual.' Picking up on June's metaphor, Ennis mentions the need to 'recharge one's batteries' and asks June to say more about what 'I am me' is like for her.

Smale, et al. (1993) have highlighted three types of assessment process:

- **The questioning model** Information gathering through finding 'facts' and collecting statements, going on to making deductions and arriving at professional judgements. This involves systematically asking questions and processing the answers informed by underpinning theory, agency policies, requirements and frameworks. In this model the social worker has an expert role.

- **The procedural model** A process dominated by frameworks, agency checklists and guides with required questions. This involves judging whether a person fits the criteria for services. Little judgement is required as the information gathered is interpreted by rules and policies that determine what should happen.

- *The exchange model.* People are viewed as experts on their difficulties and information is exchanged. What people say is not interpreted, but is used for helping them to locate inner resources and potential and for deciding how best to work together to agree goals and work on them.

Parton and O'Byrne (2000) suggest that *constructive assessment* is most closely related to the exchange model but point out that *constructive* ideas can also contribute to the questioning model.

Models based on systems theory and social exchange theory

ACTIVITY 3.1

How widespread geographically are members of your nuclear and extended family and how emotionally close are you to them?

How well do you know your neighbours?

How extensive is your circle of friends and colleagues?

What social groups do you belong to?

Comment

The answers to the above questions will differ for each one of us but they remind us that we are all part of social systems that we can envisage as an ecological framework. Systems thinking is the understanding of a phenomenon within the context of a larger whole. To understand things systemically literally means to put them into a context, to establish the nature of their relationships.

Systemic and ecological approaches

Consider the central-heating system in a building. To understand the phenomenon of a room being too cold we need to understand the whole system and where the problem might be located. You are a neurobiological system and if you have a headache you might look within yourself, or at external factors influencing you, or at a combination of these, to understand why you are feeling as you do.

Using the ecology of nature as an analogy, you can apply an ecological framework to examine the interaction between the systems that are important to service users and, for that matter, to you as a social worker.

Bronfenbrenner (1979) devised a model of environmental influences on human development depicted as concentric circles with the individual person at the centre. Around the person are micro, meso, exo and macro systems of influence.

- The *microsystem* around a person consists of their identity influenced by relationships with their immediate family and significant others.

- The *mesosystem* is made up of the interacting microsystems of extended family, neighbours, friends, school, work, leisure, religious and other social groups influencing social roles and social identity.

- The *exosystem* contains micro- and mesosystems and includes the social infrastructure of education, labour market, health and medical services public transport, social services and other organisations.

- *Macrosystems* are blueprints of all the other systems and are influenced by overarching institutional patterns, including culture, customs, social policies and government initiatives, legislation and socio-economic systems.

CASE STUDY

Tamsin's family assessment

Tamsin, a social worker in a children's services team, is assessing a family consisting of Sally (28), who has a ten-year-old son Liam from a previous relationship, and has been living with Jack (29) for most of the past four years. They have a two-year-old daughter, Becky. The referral expressed concerns about Liam due to his poor school attendance, disruptive and aggressive behaviour, and apparent lack of boundaries.

Sally and Jack have an unstable relationship. He has been unemployed recently and there are considerable rent arrears. The house, which is in a poor state of repair and cleanliness, is in a run-down area of town lacking sources of support and resources.

Using the Framework for the assessment of children in need and their families (discussed in Chapter 6), Tamsin assesses Liam's development needs, Sally and Jack's parenting capacity and, in keeping with the framework's ecological model, the wider family and environmental factors, including family history and functioning, housing, employment, education, income and community resources.

Tamsin talks to Liam about himself and his relationship with his parents, assessing his identity within this household. She enquires about any wider family and friends. With the parents' consent, she contacts the school and, as well as obtaining information about Liam's behaviour, she discusses with them their policies on exclusion and dealing with challenging behaviour. The school's policy and dedicated staff able to deal with social issues may lead Tamsin to work with them rather than assess the need for solely direct intervention from her. Knowledge of social policy relating to issues such as poverty and social exclusion help her understand this family in its wider context.

As a social worker using a systemic perspective you would take account of environmental factors in your model of assessment. A social worker such as Tamsin in the above case study may use an eco map (Parker and Bradley, 2007, Chapter 2), drawing the service users in the centre with lines linking them to their network of relationships and influence. Bold, dotted and irregular lines can depict strong, weak and troubled relationships respectively to illustrate sources of support or conflict. As part of an assessment you can analyse personal social support networks according to size, proximity, stability, frequency of contact and density.

Resilience factors that help individuals overcome early negative experiences, survive under pressure and recover from trauma (Gilligan, 2001) relate to wider family and environmental networks. They include enduring relationships outside the household such as grandparents and teachers; recognition and achievement, through educational and sporting achievement; positive family relationships; and minimising social risk factors.

The positive influences of wider systems have been conceptualised as *social capital* (Woolcock, 2001) and include citizenship, neighbourliness, trust and shared values, community involvement, civic participation and social networks.

Social exchange theory

American sociologist Homans (1958) was one of the earliest theorists to put forward ideas about social behaviour as a process of negotiated exchanges and reciprocity between people. Borrowing ideas from economics, social exchange theory suggests that human relationships are influenced by a subjective cost–benefit analysis. Individuals weigh up what they perceive as the cost of a relationship against the perceived benefits and may choose to leave the relationship if they feel that the benefits outweigh the costs. Although the theory is often applied to intimate relationships and has been used to explain conflict in conjugal relationships (Bagarozzi and Wodarski, 1977), it can provide insights for any social exchange.

The give and take of relationships is a salutary reminder of power issues. A service user being assessed, who perceives the social worker as a powerful interrogator who is part of a wider system with all the knowledge and control of resources, may feel they are giving information about themselves under pressure from a position of weakness.

The *exchange model* of assessment has already highlighted that information is exchanged between social worker and service user. The service user is likely to perceive benefits in the exchange if the social worker views them as an expert on themselves and does not interpret what they say but uses the information to understand the person and their strengths as well as their concerns and difficulties.

C H A P T E R S U M M A R Y

In this chapter we explored ways in which theory informs the practice of undertaking social work assessments. Having considered the role of theory itself, we accepted there is no single theory for assessment, but rather a variety of theoretical underpinning.

Using three broad categories, the chapter firstly introduced psychological theories such as psychodynamic approaches suggesting that unconscious motives influence behaviour; we saw that different attachment patterns can influence the behaviour not only of children but also of adults either positively or negatively; we considered the development of internal cognitive processes; a behavioural approach suggested that behaviour is learned through conditioning; and humanistic insights highlighted the potential of humans to grow into fully functioning persons. Acknowledging the role of social learning led to exploring a cognitive behavioural approach to encourage service users to work on their own faulty cognitions, ways of thinking and flawed reasoning. Other perspectives included a task-centred approach to social work used to agree goals to work on jointly with a service user in a short period of time; and a solution-focused approach building on people's resources and coping strategies.

To balance the theoretical approaches in the previous category, we secondly considered post-modernist perspectives that challenge the nature of knowledge, seeing it as socially constructed. This led to accepting the service user's own narrative as their reality and a constructive social work approach focusing on people's strengths. Considering the questioning, procedural and exchange models of assessment, we saw that the exchange model accepted people as experts on themselves.

Thirdly, ecological models based on systems theory showed us the importance of understanding individuals in the context of their wider family and environmental factors, linking with the concepts of resilience and social capital. Social exchange theory provided a reminder of the give and take and power differential in assessment, suggesting ways of equalising your relationship with the person being assessed.

FURTHER READING

Howe, D (2009) *A brief introduction to social work theory.* Basingstoke: Palgrave Macmillan.
This is a new text providing an excellent brief introduction to theories underpinning social work practice. It reviews the ones mentioned in this chapter and more.

Milner, J and O'Byrne, P (2009) *Assessment in social work.* 3rd edition. Basingstoke: Palgrave Macmillan.
A new edition of a well-established text on social work assessment, it has chapters outlining psychodynamic, behavioural, task-centred, solution-focused and narrative approaches.

Payne, M (2005) *Modern social work theory.* 3rd edition. Basinstoke: Palgrave Macmillan.
In addition to being a useful introduction to post-modernism and social construction, this text reviews most theoretical perspectives introduced in this chapter from a critical viewpoint.

Chapter 4
Values underpinning assessment

This chapter will help you to meet the following National Occupational Standards:

Key Role 1: Prepare for and work with individuals, families, carers, groups and communities to assess their needs and circumstances.

- Work with individuals, families, carers, groups and communities to help them make informed decisions.
- Assess needs and options to recommend a course of action.

Key Role 2: Plan, carry out, review and evaluate social work practice with individuals, families, carers, groups and communities and other professionals.

- Address behaviour which presents a risk to individuals, families, carers, groups and communities.

Key Role 3: Support individuals to represent their needs, views and circumstances.

- Advocate with, and on behalf of, individuals, families, carers, groups and communities.

Key Role 5: Understand what is involved in managing and accountability, with supervision and support, of your own social work practice within your organisation.

- Manage and be accountable for your own work.

Key Role 6: Demonstrate professional competence in social work practice.

- Manage complex ethical issues, dilemmas and conflicts that might affect your practice.

It will also introduce you to the following academic standards as set out in the social work subject benchmark statement:

5.1.3 Values and ethics.

- The moral concepts of rights, responsibility, freedom, authority and power inherent in the practice of social workers as moral and statutory agents.
- The complex relationships between justice, care and control in social welfare and the practical and ethical implications of these, including roles as statutory agents and in upholding the law in respect of discrimination.
- Aspects of philosophical ethics relevant to the understanding and resolution of value dilemmas and conflicts in both interpersonal and professional contexts.
- The conceptual links between codes defining ethical practice, the regulation of professional conduct and the management of potential conflicts generated by the codes held by different professional groups.

Problem-solving skills.

5.5.3 Analysis and synthesis.

- Assess human situations, taking into account a variety of factors (including the views of participants, theoretical concepts, research evidence, legislation and organisational policies and procedures).

- Consider specific factors relevant to social work practice (such as risk, rights, cultural differences and linguistic sensitivities, responsibilities to protect vulnerable individuals and legal obligations).
- Analyse and take account of the impact of inequality and discrimination in work with people in particular contexts and problem situations.
- **5.6 Communication skills**.
- Listen actively to others, engage appropriately with the life experiences of service users, understand accurately their viewpoint and overcome personal prejudices to respond appropriately to a range of complex personal and interpersonal situations.
- Communicate effectively across potential barriers resulting from differences (for example, in culture, language and age).

Introduction

In Chapters 2 and 3 we considered skills and areas of theoretical knowledge that are used in assessment. We now move on to explore values that underpin your professional practice.

What we value in life can be diverse. Parents may value a low-cost ornament bought by a child with pocket money. The value is in the meaning of the gesture that represents love. Some people may value having spent a large amount of money to buy a house because it represents a secure home. To others such a purchase may mean status, it may represent an investment, or a way of making more money by selling it at a profit. Football clubs may value the skills and popularity of a player, leading them to spend millions on a transfer deal. Many may value the help of a nurse or personal carer although their pay is relatively low.

Values involve principles relating to our judgement about what is valuable or important in life.

ACTIVITY **4.1**

- *What do you consider to be the difference between personal and professional values?*
- *List some of your personal values.*
- *List some professional social work values.*
- *Is there an overlap between the above two?*

Comment

You may have listed personal values that underpin what you are or do – being generous, a vegetarian or recycling waste. These values relate to principles you live by, although as a social worker you would not impose them on your service users. However, there are values such as respecting other people and property and not using racial or other forms of abusive language that are expected of us as professional social workers and may overlap with our personal values. We also expect service users to abide by some of these, as evidenced by signs to this effect in reception areas and waiting rooms of social work offices.

As a qualified social worker you are required to register with the General Social Care Council (GSCC) and work to its Codes of Practice. You may also be guided by other codes of ethics and textbooks about social work values. When you assess someone, the values underpinning such codes will guide how you behave towards them, how you deal with the information they give you and how you cope with problematic situations and conflicts of interest. As a professional, you are required to undertake every aspect of social work assessment in an ethical way.

We might say then that social work values are principles or standards highlighting what is valuable or important in professional practice, which lead us to behave in ethical (morally correct, honourable) ways.

An American Jesuit priest who taught social work, Father Felix Biestek (1957), published a book that became very influential. He set out seven principles arising from needs of clients:

1. *Individualisation* – to be treated as an individual.

2. *Purposeful expression of feelings* – to express feelings freely, especially negative feelings.

3. *Controlled emotional involvement* – to get a sympathetic response to problems.

4. *Acceptance* – to be recognised as a person of worth.

5. *Non-judgemental attitude* – not to be judged. Casework excludes assigning a degree of responsibility for causation of problems or needs.

6. *Client self-determination* – to make own choices and decisions.

7. *Confidentiality* – to keep secrets about oneself.

Written over 50 years ago and not explicitly as a values and ethics textbook, it is still valid and evidence that social work in the West has a value base influenced by Judeo-Christian roots and works to principles that involve accepting every individual as a person of worth and respecting them as a fellow human being. Social workers at times have to deal with complex ethical issues. Their work is governed by codes of practice, as well as professional values, and by powers and duties enshrined in legislation. Such fundamental principles are the foundations of a large, and at times unwieldy, social work edifice.

In September 2002 the GSCC launched codes of practice for social care workers and employers. A condition of GSCC registration is to abide by the codes. The codes (GSCC, 2004) state that as a social care worker you must:

1. *Protect the rights and promote the interests of service users and carers*. Treating each person as an individual; promoting individual views, supporting service users to make informed choices and respecting their dignity and privacy.

2. *Strive to establish and maintain the trust and confidence of service users.* Respecting confidential information and being professional.

3. *Promote the independence of service users while protecting them as far as possible from danger and harm.*

4. *Respect the rights of service users while seeking to ensure that their behaviour does not harm themselves or other people.* Recognising that service users have the right to take risks.

5. *Uphold public trust and confidence in social care services.* Not abusing, exploiting or discriminating against service users and carers.

6. *Be accountable for the quality of your work and take responsibility for maintaining and improving your knowledge and skills.*

In April 2002 The British Association of Social Workers (BASW) launched its new Code of Ethics for Social Work. The code adopts a value-based international definition of social work issued by the International Federation of Social Workers and the International Association of Schools of Social Work.

> *The social work profession promotes social change, problem solving in human relationships and the empowerment and liberation of people to enhance well-being. Utilising theories of human behaviour and social systems, social work intervenes at the points where people interact with their environments. Principles of human rights and social justice are fundamental to social work.*

> (2001, p1)

BASW goes on to outline that social work is committed to five basic values:

- human dignity and worth;
- social justice;
- service to humanity;
- integrity;
- competence.

Social work practice should both promote respect for *human dignity* and pursue *social justice*, through *service to humanity, integrity and competence.*

The code outlines principles arising from each value. While these values and principles apply only to social workers that join the association and become members of BASW, they are generally accepted as a code that every social worker would be expected to follow.

You will probably agree that Biestek's fundamental principles are reflected in the underpinning values forming the basis of the Codes of Practice and Code of Ethics. The codes also introduce some wider considerations and responsibilities.

Values therefore have implications for and lead to principles about:

- the personal impact of being an assessor on you and on the person you are assessing;

- having duties and responsibilities particularly to your employing agency but also towards the social work profession and society;

- accepting an individual as a person of worth and assessing their unique needs;

- respecting diversity;

- the constraints in social work of observing confidentiality.

We will now explore some of the complexity of these areas.

Being an assessor

Comment

You probably agree that a person being assessed will be anxious and apprehensive. You might also be apprehensive, particularly as a student and early on in your career, and you will want to take your responsibilities seriously by behaving professionally and ethically.

As an assessor you will be interacting with people and being guided by the values and principles outlined at the beginning of this chapter. This is different from, say, a doctor making a diagnosis, a psychologist using psychometric tests to measure attributes such as intelligence, aptitude and personality, or a university tutor marking your assignment.

Although as a social worker you will sometimes use frameworks or questionnaires, these should not lead you to placing the person in a certain category or labelling them as part of a group. You will be involving the person in discussion of what their needs are rather than making a judgement on how eloquently they speak up for themselves or measuring them against their knowledge of resources available.

In the role of assessor you will have power, which you must not misuse. You will have professional power; there is power in being the representative of an agency such as a local authority; you have legal powers and duties; and you will almost certainly be less vulnerable than the person you are assessing.

Beckett and Maynard (2006, p115) discuss professional power and say

> *Social workers' control of access to services and resources can also give them considerable power. Service users may be expected to submit to a complex and intrusive assessment process administered by social workers in order to be considered for such services and resources, and the social worker's analysis of their needs may be crucial in determining whether or not they are successful in obtaining them.*

The term *to submit* to an assessment is a significant one that suggests surrendering or yielding to authority. As a social worker you should be aware of how you are likely to be perceived by service users.

CASE STUDY

Karin was a student in her first statutory practice placement with a learning disability team. Following some joint observation visits with other practitioners, she was undertaking an assessment herself for the first time. Her practice assessor went with her to conduct a direct observation. Karin was assessing Dawn, who has Down's syndrome, lives on her own and works at a local supermarket. Karin felt anxious, and asking Dawn questions reminded her of her selection interview for the social work programme when she had been very nervous.

Karin was aware of degree teaching about the government's Valuing People initiatives promoting choice and independence. She tried not to use jargon that Dawn may not understand but, as the interview went on, that made it very difficult for her to ask some of the questions in the Care Management assessment form based on eligibility criteria. At one point Karin felt overwhelmed and resorted to mechanically reading the questions from the form rather than trying to engage Dawn in conversation. Dawn mentioned a boyfriend who came round a lot and suggested she was not happy about this. Karin moved on to the next question, feeling too embarrassed to ask Dawn about that relationship, whether it was a sexual one and Dawn's awareness of safe sex guidelines. Dawn wanted information about a college course on computing and advice about physical exercise. She did not have needs that would meet the agency's eligibility criteria and Karin was concerned about this as she thought Dawn needed guidance and advice.

Immediately after the visit Karin felt emotionally and physically drained. Discussing the assessment with her assessor, Karin was largely negative about herself, but the assessor pointed out some of her positive communication skills, particularly towards the beginning of the interview, as well as some assessment skills that she would have to work on as she gained experience and confidence.

Assessment involves gathering personal information, which may seem intrusive, analysing that information and going on to make decisions that may involve ethically difficult situations. These can impact on you as an assessor, as McAuliffe (2005) states, *positively or negatively, at a number of levels, and in a range of ways.* In addition to the need to be skilled in ethical decision making, McAuliffe stresses *the importance of professional support and supervision.*

RESEARCH SUMMARY

Donna McAuliffe (2005) outlines a qualitative study she conducted with 30 Australian social workers working with various service user groups, who explicitly stated that they had what they defined as an ethical dilemma. Examples included a service user dying of AIDS requesting that the social worker supply him with information about euthanasia, and a social worker covertly assisting a disabled mother to 'abandon' her child so that she could receive emergency respite because the service user, who felt no longer able to cope, had requested respite care that was not available due to lack of resources.

The immediate and short–medium term (defined as up to 12 months) stress responses of the social workers in this study were explored using the headings in the table below.

Short–medium term responses to the experience of an ethical dilemma included:

Emotional responses	Physiological responses	Behavioural responses
Depression Agitation and irritation Isolation/social withdrawal Overwhelmed feelings Paranoia Anger and frustration Decreased tolerance	Physical exhaustion High blood pressure Immune system problems Insomnia	Humour Physical fitness Self-care Focus on tasks Devising action plans Denial

Long-term impacts resulting from ethical dilemma are listed below with an indication as to whether they were negative (-) or positive (+) impacts.

Impacts on attitude	Impacts on awareness	Impacts on practice	Personal impacts
Cynicism about role of human service organisations (-) Acknowledgement of value of social work as a profession (+)	Political realities and power dynamics (+) Clarity of roles and responsibilities (+) Exploitation and work abuse (+) Need for self-care (+) Importance of supervision (+)	Policy and procedures (+) Social justice advocacy (+) Career promotion (-) Professional development opportunities (-) Professional reputation (-) Student assistance (+) Influence on policy (+)	Relationships (-) Career change (-)

The study shows that the highest number of ethical dilemmas related in some way to organisational policies and procedures, with social workers being caught between adhering to their personal or professional values, or complying with organisational mandates. When carrying out formal assessments you will be working to government frameworks and agency guidelines that can force you to face ethical dilemmas, such as assessing someone that does not meet eligibility criteria when you would like to offer help.

→

Having duties and responsibilities

Following consideration of what it means to be an assessor, we must now take this further and look at being an assessor as an employee of, and accountable to, a local authority or other organisation. You will be working to an agency's policies and procedures and these may at times clash with your individual or professional values as stated by McAuliffe (2005) above. If you are a statutory social worker you will also have legal powers and duties; you will at times have a legal duty to assess or investigate. Having made the assessment, you then have the responsibility to decide whether the person can have services and you may have to inform them that they do not meet the eligibility level of your local authority; at best you may direct them to another agency or organisation. It may not feel as if you are respecting the rights and promoting the interests of that person. Parrott (2006, p72) points out that *the law by itself is not value-free or objective. It embodies values of its own which reflect the power of dominant groups in society to frame and influence what the law should embody.*

Before ... when he was a lot younger, and because he'd become a Schedule 1 offender, because of whatever he'd done, he was a Schedule 1 offender, he met up with this girl, who had a baby, child protection, conference, on the register, never saw a social worker again. Right? Two years later Sandra starts working for the department and has to go out and make an assessment. And it was embarrassing. And they actually...I had to work with this family for six months, who didn't want me, and who were basically saying, 'We've never seen anybody for two years and now you turn up and you're asking all these questions.'

Sandra gives compressed information, not in sentence format, illustrating her frustration and impatience with the situation. She uses single words or short phrases to describe the familiar typical social work process: ... child protection, conference, on the register, never saw a social worker again. *It produces a sense of Sandra's feelings of being a cog in the social service wheel, just as much as the family is. She uses her name 'Sandra' to refer to herself, before using 'I' when she recounts going to see the family (she had no choice), emphasising feelings of powerlessness, being subject to the command of a higher authority. The account does not present the teller as an active moral agent, able to make a choice.*

You are accountable to the agency that employs you, but you are also accountable to the person you are assessing. In the example above, Sandra says she is embarrassed at times. After further clarification from the interviewer, she went on to agree that as the stepfather was a Schedule 1 offender there was a need to assess, but she thought the department should not expect social workers to suddenly enter into somebody else's life for their own procedures.

When informing a person you have assessed about the outcome, you should explain the decision openly and carefully and, if they do not meet eligibility criteria, you might let the person know that you do not agree with the decision you are making on behalf of your agency. You could give the person information about how to appeal against the decision within the procedures of your agency, and advocate on their behalf when they do so. Parrott (2006, p73) concludes that

> *As a social worker you are not just an employee, but a professional who has a range of responsibilities which do not begin and end with your responsibility to your employer, although this clearly constitutes one of your responsibilities.*

Beckett and Maynard (2005) see assessments as involving *advocacy versus fairness.* The reality is that any resources are finite and will have limits and this can be incompatible with promoting the interests of individuals. Should you first and foremost be an advocate for individuals, or should your primary obligation be to contribute to your agency's need to distribute its resources fairly? Beckett and Maynard (2006, p97) say

> *It seems to us that a social worker has a duty to do both these things – advocate for service users and contribute towards her agency being as fair (and non-discriminatory) as possible – but that these two duties pull in different directions.*

As well as duties towards your employing agency, which as we have seen can sometimes be in conflict with duties towards service users, you will have duties towards the social work profession and society. Codes of practice help you to maintain professional, effective and ethical practice, which includes not abusing, exploiting or discriminating against service users and carers.

When dealing with such conflicting demands it is important for you to keep accurate and up-to-date records of your actions and decisions, to have regular supervision, and to pursue training events that contribute to your continuous professional development. The need for a sensible work–life balance is also crucial.

In respecting the rights of service users you will have a duty to society, including seeking to ensure that the behaviour of people with whom you are working does not harm themselves or other people. Service users have the right to take risks but you have a duty to minimise the risks individuals may pose to themselves and to others. When gathering information for an assessment you may be told about behaviour that poses a risk and may harm an individual or others, that may be dangerous or illegal. The right of a service user to self-determination and making their own decisions and choices can conflict with the law or with the rights of other individuals.

CASE STUDY

Mona, a care manager working with older people, is visiting 87-year-old Phyllis who lives alone in a sheltered housing flat. After a period of sight deterioration, Phyllis has been completely blind for five years. She used to be a professional accountant and is proud of her independence. She has the choice of a communal evening meal but prepares snacks in her flat. Mona is assessing whether the care package should include a carer coming in to help Phyllis with lunch or at other times if needed. When Phyllis makes cups of coffee for them, Mona observes her boiling an electric kettle. She uses her hands to judge the position of the mugs to pour in the boiling water. She puts a finger on the rim of the mug to judge through the heat when the mug is close to full and she should stop pouring. Phyllis tells Mona that she can make herself cheese sandwiches. She cuts cheddar cheese with a serrated-edge knife, using her fingers to judge the thinness of the slices. She says she has once or twice made cheese on toast using her eye-level electric grill by listening to the bubbling of the cheese and smelling it to decide when it was ready. She doesn't do this very often as she is aware of the danger and she has friends and relatives that come to see her quite often and help out. Phyllis does not want an increase in her care package.

Mona decides that promoting Phyllis's independence and respecting her self-determination and her right to choose are more important than the risks that Phyllis is knowingly taking. Mona discusses all this with Phyllis and tells her that this is the decision she will record but that it can be reviewed.

Assessing the individual needs of a person

We now move on to consider that, notwithstanding the occasional conflicts explored in the previous section, a fundamental value in working with people is to accept them as individuals with unique needs and wishes, not as a typical case or a type of condition. As an assessor, accountable to your employing agency, you will endeavour to understand the person you are assessing and, together with them, to identify their individual needs. In this way you will be *person-centred* and your assessment will be *needs led*.

Being person-centred includes accepting the individual's views and feelings. Accurate empathy is needed to meaningfully understand these. Earlier in this chapter we considered power issues arising from your role as assessor. Accepting the common humanity between you and a fellow human being involves equalising the power between you and that person. It may involve enabling a vulnerable person to feel empowered to take responsibility for their own situation.

CASE STUDY

Carl has been a service user of a Community Mental Health Team for some years. He has been diagnosed as having obsessive-compulsive disorder and has had previous periods of acute depression and anxiety that resulted in hospital treatment. He has been stable for the past two years, managing his medication. He has a considerable amount of insight into his condition and discusses with Simon, his social worker, a progression from needs associated with his psychiatric condition to more social and personal needs. He would like to get a job and wonders whether there might be clerical work available where his tendency to being at times over-precise, attending to detail and making lists would be considered a strength rather than a weakness. Simon has a close working relationship with Carl and they usually meet in a local café. Although they are not personal friends, they respect each other. Simon tells Carl that his current assessment is that Carl should be working towards his case being formally closed by the team, leaving him to access help if he feels he needs it.

Through relating in this way to the person you are assessing you will be treating them as an individual, promoting their individual views, supporting them to make informed choices and respecting their dignity and privacy. Banks (2006, p29) outlines the Kantian principle of respect for persons and reminds us that

> *the individual person is intrinsically worthy of respect simply because she or he is a person, regardless of whether we like the person, whether they are useful to us or whether they have behaved badly towards us.*

From this principle follows the responsibility not to discriminate against a person for any reason and not to judge them. As a social worker you have an obligation to practise in an anti-discriminatory way, particularly towards those who are discriminated against in society. However, we are all different so anti-discriminatory practice and accepting diversity is good social work practice at any level and with any service user group.

While we can say that people who experience discrimination are oppressed, some writers (e.g. Dalrymple and Burke, 1995) have used the term anti-oppressive practice as a broader one than anti-discriminatory practice. Drawing on social theory, it implies understanding power differences embedded in society with power residing with majority social systems. Anti-oppressive practice leads social workers to challenge and confront issues on a personal and a structural level.

Ways in which you can treat people as individuals include involving them in their assessment as 'experts by experience', keeping them fully informed of your responsibilities, limitations, obligations and decisions, and allowing them choice as far as possible.

Respecting diversity

Discussion of respecting each person as an individual without discrimination leads us to consider the fact that we are all different.

ACTIVITY **4.2**

- *Think of yourself in relation to other students on your programme or colleagues at work.*
- *In what ways are you 'different'?*
- *How different are you to those closest to you personally or professionally?*

Comment

The differences you thought of may have included gender, age, background, interests, sexual orientation, disability, class, nationality, language, religion, ethnicity.

Are you less different to those closest to you? It is sometimes easier to relate to those who, due to personal characteristics or attributes, are more like us. It can be more difficult to understand someone who is different from us for various reasons. Since some groups experience particular discrimination in society, social workers must promote equality while understanding differences.

Beckett and Maynard (2005, p170) remind us that

> *The existence of difference is a challenge to our own identity. If someone makes different choices to me, does that mean my choices are wrong? If someone believes in a different god to me, aren't they calling my god into question? If someone speaks a different language, how can I be sure of what they are saying? And the same insecurities can arise when people look different, or have a different kind of body or different sexual interests.*

In social work assessment it is very important to gather accurate information and interpret it correctly. This can be very difficult when something gets in the way of us understanding the needs of a person.

In the 1970s and 1980s concern for racism emerged in the social work profession. There was an emphasis on anti-racist practice. Laird (2008, p22) points out that

> *During the 1990s the focus shifted from anti-racist practice to anti-oppressive practice and the development of a generic approach to different forms of discrimination. The shift towards anti-oppressive practice meant that other forms of discrimination on the grounds of class, disability, age, sexuality and gender were identified, together with that of racism. This meant that the interaction of different oppressions could be explored rather than only focusing on racism.*

While there are some advantages to this trend in terms of understanding aspects of discrimination and oppression, it can be counter-productive in terms of respecting diversity as it conceptualises discrimination as a homogeneous experience when social work values are that we should understand each person as an individual.

A way of respecting diversity is accepting that the values of a person we are assessing may be different from ours. Through good communication skills, showing empathy and asking another about themselves we begin to understand the other person at a meaningful level. You are not expected to be an expert on every culture. Parrott (2006, p29) reminds us that

> *Moving beyond common-sense attitudes about 'difference' requires the social worker to literally inhabit the world of the 'other'; this exercise of empathy requires deep understanding of the other person's world and their values.*

> *It also requires the social worker to reflect upon their own values and their own understanding of their identity, what privileges they have had, what struggles they have experienced.*

RESEARCH SUMMARY

Anglo-centric values

In a textbook about anti-oppressive social work, subtitled A guide for developing cultural competence, Laird (2008, pp44, 45) challenges generally assumed values derived from Western traditions, pointing out that values are different in different societies and cultures. She refers to Dwivedi (2004, p19), Lau (2004, p94) and Leininger and McFarland (2002, p109) identifying values which underpin social expectations and lifestyles in Western countries and are evident in the dominant norms of British society:

- *separation and individuation;*

- *independence;*

- *autonomy;*

→

- *self-sufficiency;*
- *competitiveness;*
- *self-expression;*
- *assertiveness;*
- *achievement oriented;*
- *immediate action;*
- *technological dependency;*
- *reliance on positivist science;*
- *materialism.*

African-centred values
As a contrast, Graham (2002, pp107–9), in her comprehensive overview of African-centredness, identifies a number of important values.
Survival of Black families *They have endured the processes of enslavement, colonisation and racism and yet remain foundational to communities of African descent.*
Strong religious and spiritual orientation *Spirituality, whether within the context of established churches or not, contributes to the resilience of the family.*
Strong achievement orientation *Black families place emphasis on the importance of education and reject the limitations placed on their children by the education system.*
Strong kinship bonds *Historically in African societies all family members, including older siblings, took part in parenting. The notion of family embraces those who are not biologically related and is open to community involvement.*
Tradition of communal self-help *Based on the principle of reciprocity, community-based groups facilitate mutual assistance among their membership.*
Adaptability of family roles to new environments *Flexibility in family roles and the sharing of responsibility to meet the needs of the family as a whole.*

Parham (2002) has written about counselling models for African Americans, some of which is transferable to UK social work. Regarding assessment, he suggests (p105):

> In assessing the psychological aspects of African descent people, care should be taken to avoid too much focus on identifying pathology and psychological debilitations rather than a more balanced approach that recognizes more positive aspects like strength, resilience, and resourcefulness. Consequently, beyond the traditional methods of assessment, it is important ... to use our inherent sensitivities to better understand our clients (Paniagua, 2000). Also, we must both acknowledge and gauge the unspoken words, the unexpressed emotions in their body language, and the unconscious attitudes and beliefs expressed in their behaviors.

In this section on diversity we have focused on African-centred values. There is no space to explore value implications of other aspects of diversity. What we have considered reminds us that there is a danger in accepting what Banks (2008) refers to as *universally valid, abstract principles, promoting individual freedoms and rights that apply worldwide across all cultures.* African-centred values are nearer to *'new'* approaches to social work ethics that Banks (2008, p1243) points out *pay attention to the situated nature of values and conduct, as embedded in families, relationships, communities, motives and emotions.* Banks suggests

> *they may offer more scope, therefore, to respond to the critique of the dominance of Western (particularly Anglo-American) approaches to ethics, which place the individual moral agent in the centre of the picture, rationally weighing up the balance of individual duties and rights.*

Observing confidentiality

Not divulging information given by someone you are working with is a common principle of professional practice and expected of doctors, lawyers and priests. Biestek's (1957) last principle reminds us of the right of individuals to privacy. The second GSCC code of practice states social workers should strive to establish and maintain the trust and confidence of service users.

For social workers, observing confidentiality is not straightforward. When you are assessing someone, you are likely to write most of the information down, put it in a report and enter it into records. Service users have a right to access their files. We mentioned the importance of support and supervision earlier and for that to take place you will share information with the person supervising your work. Social work increasingly consists of multi-agency working, and for partnership with other agencies to be meaningful there must be good communication and information sharing. It is important to work in partnership with service users by explaining procedures and considerations to them and showing them anything that you write about them.

The implications of such arrangements and expectations are that you should make the person you are assessing aware of them and explain that confidentiality does not apply personally to you but to a team, to an agency or to a group of agencies working in partnership. It would be unethical to divulge information given by one service user to another. This can be so even when working with families. You may not disclose what one parent or child says to other members of the family. Sharing information with other professionals must be done sensitively and only communicate the information that they need to know.

CASE STUDY

Melissa and Patsy

Melissa's parenting skills are improving and Susan, her social worker, assesses that she is coping quite well with Patsy who is now 18 months old. During a visit Melissa asks Susan, 'Can I tell you something in confidence?' Susan explains that, depending on what it is, she will not be able to keep it to herself because of her commitments to her local

→

CASE STUDY *continued*

authority children and families team and to other professionals and agencies involved in work with the family. Melissa accepts this as she and Susan have a relationship based on trust and tells Susan that she has developed a close friendship with a local man and is considering asking him to move in with them. This is an important piece of information that Susan could not have kept secret. She needs to find out more about this man and his relationship with Melissa, and assess the impact of his joining the household. She may share basic factual information with other agencies but not some of the more personal details that Melissa tells her.

C H A P T E R   S U M M A R Y

This chapter introduced you to underpinning values in assessment and, after exploring what values are, it clarified that values are principles or standards highlighting what is valuable or important in professional practice, which lead us to behave in ethical ways. We reviewed Biestek's fundamental principles of practice, the GSCC Codes of Practice and BASW Code of Ethics.

The chapter then encouraged you to consider the personal impact of being an assessor on you and on the person you are assessing; having duties and responsibilities particularly to your employing agency but also towards the social work profession and society; accepting an individual as a person of worth and assessing their unique needs; respecting diversity; and the constraints in social work of observing confidentiality.

FURTHER READING

Banks, S (2006) *Ethics and values in social work.* 3rd edition. London: Palgrave Macmillan.
This is an excellent introduction to professional ethics in relation to social work practice. It explores the theoretical underpinning of ethics and values.

Beckett, C and Maynard, A (2006) *Values and ethics in social work: An introduction.* London: Sage Publications.
A very helpful and accessible introduction, it starts generally exploring the nature of values and moves to more specific discussion of values and social work and to applying values in practice.

Parrott, L (2010) *Values and ethics in social work practice.* 2nd edition. Exeter: Learning Matters.
This is a book that explores the application of values and ethics to contemporary social work practice situations involving ethical conflict and dilemmas. It has a good theoretical base.

Laird, S E (2008) *Anti-oppressive social work: A guide for developing cultural competence.* London: Sage Publications.
This guide to working competently with different cultures starts by exploring racism and ethnic minorities, including some social policy implications. It updates traditional anti-discriminatory practice ideas and has chapters about communities with roots in India, Pakistan and Bangladesh, the Caribbean, China, and economic migrants and refugees.

Chapter 5
Risk assessment

A C H I E V I N G   A   S O C I A L   W O R K   D E G R E E

This chapter will help you to meet the following National Occupational Standards:

Key Role 1: Prepare for and work with individuals, families, carers, groups and communities to assess their needs and circumstances.

- Assess needs and options to recommend a course of action.

Key Role 2: Plan, carry out, review and evaluate social work practice with individuals, families, carers, groups and communities and other professionals.

- Address behaviour which presents a risk to individuals, families, carers, groups and communities.

Key Role 4: Manage risk to individuals, families, carers, groups and communities, self and colleagues.

- Assess and manage risks to individuals, families, carers, groups and communities.
- Assess, minimise and manage risk to self and colleagues.

Key Role 5: Manage and be accountable, with supervision and support, for your own social work practice within your organisation.

- Work with multi-disciplinary and multi-organisational teams, networks and systems.

Key Role 6: Demonstrate professional competence in social work practice.

- Manage complex ethical issues, dilemmas and conflicts that might affect your practice.

It will also introduce you to the following academic standards as set out in the social work subject benchmark statement:

5.1.4 Social work theory.

- The relevance of sociological perspectives to understanding societal and structural influences on human behaviour at individual, group and community levels.
- Models and methods of assessment, including factors underpinning the selection and testing of relevant information, the nature of professional judgement and the processes of risk assessment.

Problem-solving skills.

5.5.3 Analysis and synthesis.

- Assess human situations, taking into account a variety of factors (including the views of participants, theoretical concepts, research evidence, legislation and organisational policies and procedures).
- Consider specific factors relevant to social work practice (such as risk, rights, cultural differences and linguistic sensitivities, responsibilities to protect vulnerable individuals and legal obligations).

5.5.4 Intervention and evaluation.

- Undertake practice in a manner that promotes the well-being and protects the safety of all parties.

Introduction

This chapter focuses on assessment of risk in social work. We will initially explore how ideas about risk are regarded in society generally and then move on to consider risk in social work. We will see that what we mean by risk and ways of assessing it are not always straightforward and can involve ethically difficult situations, balancing rights and responsibilities.

ACTIVITY **5.1**

Briefly and in your own words write down:

- *what risk means to you;*
- *examples of risks that you have faced in your life;*
- *aspects of risk that you have come across mentioned in the media;*
- *examples of risk assessment of which you are aware.*

Comment

Did you think of risk as a chance or possibility of danger, injury or some undesirable outcome? You were probably able to draw on a variety of ideas and experiences. Slight or major personal risks may be physical, emotional, financial. You may have 'spread your risks' to minimise loss when saving or investing money. In the media we read and hear about financial risk management and analysis, and we note society's responses to terrorism or environmental threats. You may have thought about risks at work or concerning children. The Health and Safety Executive expects employers to identify hazards on work premises, evaluate risks and decide on precautions. School-teachers are required to make a risk assessment of activities, particularly if they involve taking children for a visit or trip.

At university you can do a degree on the sociology of risk and uncertainty, and responses to risk within various social contexts are the subject of academic research.

What do we mean by risk?

Risk, which can be a noun (e.g. 'there is a risk that a tragedy is going to happen') or a verb (e.g. 'they risked their lives taking part in dangerous activities'), is usually associated with a hazard or bad consequence. Although the word originally related to positive as well as negative outcomes, it is almost always now used to refer to unwelcome events. That is how the term is used in this chapter – the likelihood of something bad happening.

Risk society

Sociologists such as Ulrich Beck (1992) and Anthony Giddens (1998) have suggested we live in a 'risk society', a main characteristic of it being risk as a result of human activity and how it should be managed. Beck (1992) argues that modern civilisation can be divided into pre-industrial society, industrial society and global risk society. Giddens (1998) points out that in the Middle Ages and in traditional cultures there was no concept of risk: our current preoccupation with risk is a developing modern phenomenon. He uses the term 'reflexive modernity' to explain how individuals inter-act with society and are forced to reflect, use their judgement and make decisions in a way that was not previously required. We have to respond to risks and hazards (such as genetically modified foods and climate change) that have emerged as by-products of science, technology and industry.

A related concept is that we live in a blame culture in which businesses and organisa-tions are unwilling to take risks or accept responsibility for mistakes for fear of criticism or prosecution. In Western cultures it is far more common now for individuals to sue organisations as a result of injury or harm that might have been accepted as an unfortunate accident years ago.

Sociologist Frank Furedi has challenged many of the above ideas in a number of publications. In a provocatively titled book, *Paranoid parenting: Why ignoring the experts may be best for your child*, Furedi (2008) encourages parents not to be guided by the dangerousness of hazards in the home, other people, school, the community and environment, but to have the confidence to bring up self-assured, imaginative and capable children by allowing them to take risks. Furedi and Bristow (2008) criticise child protection policies and the increasing need for non-professionals to be cleared by the Criminal Record Bureau (CRB) and a new Independent Safeguarding Authority (ISA). They argue these requirements have made adults scared of interacting with children and policies have poisoned the relationship between the generations, creat-ing an atmosphere of suspicion that actually increases the risks to children. One of the writers recounts (pxi):

> *My daughter is allowed to play out in the street with kids from the neighbourhood. She said she was going to Semih's house and I said OK. Ten minutes later Semih's mom knocked at my door and said, 'I must introduce myself as we haven't met.' I thought she was going to tell me her name, have a chat, but she said she was CRB checked and her husband was CRB checked and then went away. I still don't know her name!*

Webb (2006) has written about social and political perspectives of social work in a risk society. He points out that the early origins of social work are rooted in the nineteenth century when insurance against insecurity at an individual and then at a government and society level developed. The legislation that led to the establishment of a welfare state was intended to provide security for citizens against the hazards produced by lack of or inadequate income, health care, educational opportunities, adequate hous-ing and gainful employment. We have experienced a shift from a 'welfare (no risk) society' to the 'risk society'. Kemshall (2007, p153) adds that *within the risk society protection is only afforded to the citizen in exceptional cases, and welfare is residual rather than universal.*

Risk in social work

Brearley (1982) was one of the first writers to highlight the concept of risk and responses to it in social work, pointing out the influence of public criticism such as that experienced after the death of Maria Colwell in 1973. He highlighted different approaches to the concept of risk, including

> *Statistical and mathematical probability models; commercial insurance approaches to risk evaluation and estimation; ideas about uncertainty in the decision analysis field; psychological measures of behaviour in situations perceived as risky; and models for the identification and balancing of risks in scientific and technological developments.*

> (p6)

Parsloe (1999) edited a textbook on risk assessment in social care and social work, with chapters about assessing risk relating to different service user groups including offenders, mental health, children and old people.

In more recent years Kemshall (2002, 2007, 2008) has prolifically addressed risk assessment and management in her research and publications. She points out that

> *One way of analysing risks in social work is to separate them into two categories:*

> * *Those risks which people pose to others.*
> * *Those risks to which people are exposed; these are perhaps best understood as referring to people who are vulnerable to risk.*
> (Kemshall, 2008, p140)

Assessing risk

One way of assessing risk has roots in actuarial estimates for the pricing of insurance. Actuaries mathematically analyse the frequency and severity of losses based on what has occurred in the past. Motor insurance premiums are higher for young people, typically under 21, because road accident figures show that statistically more young people are involved in accidents, and thus the likelihood of the insurance company incurring a cost is higher. Life assurance premiums increase as people get older because the statistical chance of someone dying, and the company having to pay a death benefit, is higher as a person grows older. Following floods in the north and southwest of England in the summer of 2007 there were reports from the British Insurance Brokers Association that places where flooding is more likely had their insurance premiums raised to unaffordable levels or that people in flood areas could become uninsurable.

Actuaries assess risk using statistics and apply probability theory, describing the likely occurrence of an event, as in working out gambling odds. The chances each time you toss a coin that the result will be 'heads' or 'tails' is 50:50, or equal probabilities of 0.5. A rare event has a probability close to 0; a very common event has a probability close to 1. When looking at research data you may sometimes see the results followed by, say, p < (or =) 0.05. That means that the probability (p) that the result could have happened by pure chance is less than (<) or sometimes equal to (=) 0.05, i.e. 5% or 1 in 20. Depending on the subject of research and the sample population there are statistical tests that can be used to show whether the results are statistically significant.

RESEARCH SUMMARY

Haines and Case (2005) evaluated a multi-agency, multiple-intervention Promoting Prevention initiative to prevent youth offending in Swansea using a self-administered computer-based interactive questionnaire with 580 young people aged 11 to 18. The group comprised almost equal numbers of males and females. The initiative included social services interventions, family–school relationships and mentoring. Results indicated that multiple exposure to family risk factors significantly increases the likelihood that a young person will become involved in offending. Exposure to multiple protective factors decreases the likelihood of problem behaviours.

The researchers used a 'Chi-square' (χ^2) statistical analysis to measure differences between young people who admitted ever offending and young people who stated they had never offended.

Offender / non-offender differences in perceptions of family factors				
Risk factor	*Overall %*	*Non-offenders %*	*Offenders %*	*$\chi2$*
Parental criminality	*36*	*24*	*44*	*24.305a*
Marital discord	*18*	*15*	*21*	*3.410*
Harsh, erratic discipline	*14*	*10*	*17*	*5.915b*
Poor communication	*13*	*14*	*13*	*0.161*
Poor supervision	*12*	*7*	*15*	*9.258c*
Unclear rules for behaviour	*11*	*11*	*12*	*0.128*
Lack of consultation	*11*	*8*	*12*	*2.305*
Poor child–parent relationship	*4*	*3*	*5*	*2.460*
Parents drink	*4*	*4*	*4*	*0.065*
Parental drug use	*3*	*2*	*3*	*0.979*
Siblings drink	*3*	*3*	*2*	*0.384*
Sibling criminality	*1*	*–*	*–*	*1.889*
Sibling drug use	*1*	*0*	*1*	*1.268*

a p<0.001
b p<0.05
c p<0.01

→

RESEARCH SUMMARY *continued*

The above table shows that while offenders perceived that they experienced more of almost all the risk factors than the non-offenders, the differences in parental criminality, harsh, erratic discipline and poor supervision were statistically significant, with parental criminality being the most significant and harsh, erratic discipline the least so.

The research helped the initiative target the appropriate factors through its interventions. This study gives evidence of factors that are predictors of delinquency, thus increasing the risk of offending for young people who experience them. It does not show that any particular young person who experienced those factors would definitely commit offences.

An alternative, or complementary, approach to actuarial assessment is clinical assessment. Kemshall (2008, p142) describes it as

> *an individualized assessment method carried out by practitioners on a case-by-case basis and essentially a diagnostic technique derived from mental health and medical fields.*

Using a clinical approach to assess the risk of a particular young person reoffending, a practitioner would assess individual and social factors based on knowledge of the family circumstances, personal contact and interviews with the young person and significant others. The practitioner would use this information to make a judgement about the risk of the young person reoffending.

In scientific medicine, trials are often conducted to evaluate the effectiveness and safety of new medication or treatment. They sometimes begin with animal trials and progress on to larger-scale studies with humans. The term 'clinical risk' is used to indicate the risk that the clinical trials may not show the intended benefits, that harm may occur, or that there may be unwanted side effects for the patients.

Clinical assessment tends to apply to an individual person or situation and is dependent on a variety of factors involved in the interaction between a social worker and service user and inevitably has a subjective element. The conclusion reached does not help to assess the risk to other individuals.

Risk assessments based on actuarial or statistical approaches give a measure of the likelihood of risk, often expressed as a percentage, but they do not definitely predict that a particular individual will experience something negative, only that they are more likely to do so. Whether they do or not will depend on a number of variable factors that can be explored through clinical assessment.

We can see then that the assessment of risk is not simple, rarely uncomplicated and is by no means infallible. As Banks (2006, p23) says, *risk assessment in social work is not a precise, scientific or straightforward business.*

Social work competence

You will know that the National Occupational Standards for Social Work comprise six key roles subdivided into 21 units of competence. Within Key Role 2 (*Plan, carry out, review and evaluate social work practice with individuals, families, carers, groups, communities and other professionals*), unit 9 requires social workers to *address behaviour which presents a risk to individuals, families, carers, groups and communities,* which includes taking immediate action to deal with the behaviour that presents a risk and work with service users to prevent and change the behaviour.

Key Role 4 (*Manage risk to individuals, families, carers, groups, communities, self and colleagues*) is subdivided into two units. Unit 12 requires social workers to *assess and manage risks to individuals, families, carers, groups and communities,* which involves identifying and assessing the nature of the risk, balancing the rights and responsibilities of service users, and regularly monitoring, reassessing and managing risk.

Unit 13 requires social workers to *assess, minimise and manage risk to self and colleagues,* including assessing potential risk to self and colleagues, working within the risk assessment and management procedures of your own and other relevant organisations and professions, and planning, monitoring and reviewing outcomes and actions to minimise stress and risk.

While there are some overlapping factors among the above requirements, this chapter addresses the assessment of risk to service users more than assessing risk to yourself and colleagues. The inclusion of risk in the standards that social workers are expected to achieve, to the extent that one of the six key roles involves managing risk, is evidence of the importance of this area to social work practice.

Another indication of the importance of risk is that the General Social Care Council (GSCC, 2004) Codes of Practice also devote one of their six codes for social care workers to practice involving risk. Code 4 states that

> *As a social care worker, you must respect the rights of service users while seeking to ensure that their behaviour does not harm themselves or other people. This includes*
>
> *4.1 recognising that service users have the right to take risks and helping them to identify and manage potential and actual risks to themselves and others;*
>
> *4.2 following risk assessment policies and procedures to assess whether the behaviour of service users presents a risk of harm to themselves or others;*
>
> *4.3 taking necessary steps to minimise the risks of service users from doing actual or potential harm to themselves or other people; and*
>
> *4.4 ensuring that relevant colleagues and agencies are informed about the outcomes and implications of risk assessments.*

The above expectations and requirements imply that in social work practice absolute safety is not completely attainable, nor indeed desirable. Risk is not entirely undesirable due to the right of each individual human being to take risks and because risk is involved in growth, development, exploration and creativity.

Assessing risk is to some extent integral to any social work assessment. As a social worker you will be dealing with vulnerable people and in your assessments you will be engaging in a process with them that will help you understand them in relation to their environment. You should also be aware of factors that increase the likelihood of risk. Assessment will lead you to plan with the service user what you might be able to do to stabilise, improve or change the service user, their environment, or both. All these involve elements of risk.

We will now move on to explore implications for assessment arising from the four subdivisions of the GSCC code above.

The right to take risks

Consideration of assessing risk brings us back to underpinning values and principles discussed in the last chapter. As individuals we all have rights, including the right to take risks. We also have the responsibility to ensure the risks we take do not endanger other people. Helping service users and carers identify potential and actual risks to themselves and others, so that they can manage risk, will probably involve a clinical risk assessment approach.

As illustrated by the Furedi and Bristow (2008) example earlier, parents have a right to allow their children to play out in the street with other '*kids from the neighbourhood*' but they also have a responsibility to take into account that there may be some risks and that they should ensure their children's safety. Parenting styles differ. Allowing a child to play outside may depend on the child's age, the neighbourhood and the culture of local families, how well the parents know other children and their parents, whether the street they play in is a quiet no-through road or a busy one, and many other factors.

CASE STUDY

Leanne is a children and families social worker and among her caseload she has two families A and B a few miles apart within a medium-sized town. Each family has a 7-year-old daughter that has been assessed as a child in need.

The parents in Family A have had substance misuse problems and have a volatile relationship that at times results in domestic violence. Leanne has found the parents difficult to engage. They tell Leanne that their daughter Kloe is often playing out in the street until 10pm at night. Leanne has concerns about their parenting as they appear to prefer their daughter to be out of their way. Weighing up risk factors and involving the parents in a clinical assessment, Leanne advises the parents against what they are doing and discusses the dangers with them.

The parents in family B have been inconsistent in their emotional responses to their daughter Hollee and have at times provided inconsistent boundaries, but seem to be responding to advice on parenting. They had financial problems that added pressure to their relationship. They tell Leanne that Hollee goes out to play with neighbours' children in a cul-de-sac at the back of the house some days until 8.00 or 8.30pm. They leave the back door open and keep an eye on her. Leanne assesses that there is no serious risk to this practice and discusses boundaries with the parents.

The parents of both families have a right to take risks with their children but Leanne, the social worker, has a responsibility to assess the priority needs of children in need and whether, in some cases, there may be child protection considerations to take into account.

A social worker or care manager working with a learning disabled young person preparing them to live independently of their parents, or supporting a frail older person to manage independently on their own, may encourage positive risk taking in those situations.

Risk assessment policies and procedures

The scenarios in the case study above will have reminded you that the social worker has duties under legislation such as the Children Act 1989 to safeguard and promote the welfare of children in need (as defined by the Act) and to investigate whether a child is suffering or is likely to suffer significant harm. In addition to legislation, organisations also have risk assessment policies and procedures to help you as a social worker assess whether the behaviour of service users presents a risk of harm to themselves or others. These procedures, such as a children in need matrix or a vulnerable adults risk scale, tend to involve an actuarial or statistical predictive approach. Although the procedures may help you engage with service users in a 'clinical' way, they tend to outline risk factors and their severity to help you assess the likelihood of service users posing a risk to others, or service users' own vulnerability to risk.

Posing risk to others is often associated with work within criminal justice and to some extent mental health. It has been conceptualised as the assessment of 'dangerousness'. Pinard and Pagani (2000) see it as an inexact science and point out that it is dependent on many complex factors. Kemshall (2007, p140) puts forward common features of the risk assessment of people who pose a risk to others:

- *the person assessed is seen as a poser of risk to others;*
- *risk is defined as harmful behaviour, with the harm directed to others;*
- *the desired outcome of risk assessment is accurate identification of risky persons and their likely behaviours;*
- *the desired outcome of risk management is the reduction or avoidance of risk to others;*

- *the rights, and to some extent the liberty, of posers of risk can be limited in the interests of protecting others and preventing future risks.*

The last of the above bullet points is in contrast to the right to take risks discussed in the previous section and reminds us of the complexity and at times conflicting requirements and duties involved in assessment of risks.

Kemshal (2007, pp140,141) outlines key features involved in assessing exposure to risks, or a person's vulnerability.

- *Identification and assessment of the risks to which the client is exposed. What risks are they likely to encounter and with what result?*
- *Determining whether such risks are acceptable or not. Should the risks be run?*
- *Balancing the desirability of reducing risk against the likely reduction of choice and the impact upon quality of life; for example, the reduction of risk to an older person through admission to a residential care home has to be balanced against their consequent loss of independence.*
- *Risk management strategies are generally informed by the desire to balance risk reduction with autonomy, quality of life and rights.*

CASE STUDY

Edith and Frank

Edith (79) has severe arthritis and other physical problems. She finds it increasingly difficult to walk, go up stairs, cook, clean and generally go about her daily routine as she has done for many years. There have been some instances of confusion lately, such as putting the gas on but not lighting it and walking down the road in her nightdress. Her husband Frank (80) is physically well but not used to household tasks. His wife has in the past undertaken all of the housework. He finds that he has to increasingly care for Edith. Liz, a married daughter, lives nearby and comes in to help. She thinks her parents are not coping and that her mother should go into residential care. Frank wants to remain at home with his wife. Liz's husband Peter agrees with Frank and through disagreeing with Liz about her parents some tension develops in Peter and Liz's relationship.

Richard, a care manager who is aware of the wider family situation, has to remind himself that Edith is the service user. As Edith's carer, Frank is also entitled to an assessment. In assessing them, Richard has to take into account Edith and Frank's choice, the possible increasing deterioration in Edith's quality of life and independence. Richard is surprised at Frank's inability to undertake chores around the home, but he is not judgemental and accepts that has been their lifestyle. There are risks such as Edith falling or hurting herself if she attempts to be as active in the house as she used to be and risks related to her confusion. Initially a care package involving carers coming in twice a day and meals being delivered will enable Edith and Frank to manage, but this will have to be monitored and reviewed.

Minimising risks

Through agreeing a care package with Edith and Frank as suggested in the case study above, the care manager is taking necessary steps to minimise the risks of service users from doing actual or potential harm to themselves or to each other. The care manager will monitor and reassess the risks.

In what we earlier in this chapter termed a risk society, with a climate of high accountability and blame, there is a tendency by some agencies to have an inclination towards risk aversion and this can lead in children's services to too readily instituting care proceedings when there is any inkling of child neglect or abuse, and in adult services to resisting older or other vulnerable people living independently and taking increasing responsibility for their own care needs. Taking steps to minimise risks also involves the balance of risk reduction with autonomy, quality of life and rights.

Minimising risks may at times involve protecting others. In a child protection investigation a social worker must be satisfied that a victim of abuse is safe from the perpetrator.

Informing relevant colleagues and agencies

Social work is increasingly undertaken in multi-agency partnerships, so ensuring that relevant colleagues and agencies are informed about the outcomes and implications of risk assessments is essential. In a community mental health team (CMHT), for instance, your colleagues may include a psychiatrist, community psychiatric nurse (CPN), occupational therapist, clinical psychologist and pharmacist, as well as social workers. They will bring different viewpoints and the background of their disciplines to the assessment, monitoring and reassessment of risk. Although it is sometimes difficult to handle the diversity of opinions and approaches, at best there can be synergy in the contributions of different professionals.

Assessing and intervening in risky situations by their very nature involve a number of agencies such as health, police, education, voluntary and private organisations and social services. In a helpful outline of steps contributing to a secure way of approaching risk assessment, Sheldon and Macdonald (2009, p106) include:

> *Piece together the chronology of events, including contacts with other agencies, and collect information from all relevant parties. This 'picture-making' is routinely undertaken in circumstances where people have died, and typically leads to a great deal of information known to a variety of people never before put together. We are less good at it with the living and the as yet uninjured.*

Working with risk is more often than not a joint activity. The participation and contribution of each party should be clear. Sheldon and Macdonald (2009, p106) warn that *diffusion of responsibility ... can be a side-effect of the increased cooperation that all inquiry reports call for.*

> **CASE STUDY**
>
> *Margot, a social worker in a CMHT, has to assess Helen, referred by her GP following an attempted suicide. Margot visits Helen at home in a rather old and unkempt block of flats on the edge of the city. The area has limited shops, leisure and social facilities and the public transport links with the centre of the city are inadequate. Helen is 28 years old, a single parent with a four-year-old son Wayne, and she finds it difficult to manage financially on benefits. She cannot afford to go out for any social or leisure activities that involve payment and has not had a holiday for some years.*
>
> *Margot uses good communication skills to talk to Helen about her background. Helen experienced sexual abuse from her father when she was a school girl and her mother died of cancer when Helen was an adolescent. Helen had several relationships with men and separated from Wayne's father after a rather turbulent cohabitation. She feels lonely and isolated. Although living in a block of flats, she has little contact with neighbours and she is frightened of some local young people that often vandalise the property and can be abusive to local residents. She tells her narrative in a negative, self-blame way, as if much of what has happened to her is her fault. She would like to take up singing or playing the guitar in some way, something she really enjoyed at school. She has had suicide thoughts a number of times but only attempted it once by taking an overdose of anti-depressants she had from her GP. A neighbour looked after Wayne when she was in hospital overnight and a social worker from a children and families team made contact following a referral from the hospital. Helen does not find her GP helpful; he does little more than give her anti-depressants that she says make her feel lethargic.*
>
> *From this initial assessment, Margot is aware that Helen has a number of factors strongly associated with depression, increasing the risk that she might attempt suicide. Helen agrees that a CPN colleague of Margot can come to see her and complete a Depression Inventory Scale with her, and she consents to a referral to the CMHT psychiatrist for a reassessment of her anti-depressant medicine. Margot says she will keep the social worker in the children and families team informed and offers to continue contact with Helen to assess her finances, accommodation and explore sources of support. Margot offers to get information from a local MIND project that runs support groups and a drop-in centre.*

In this case example, Margot the social worker is assessing Helen's vulnerability and the risk of self-harm or suicide. She is also assessing the risk to Wayne if his mother becomes further depressed or attempts suicide again. Margot is combining actuarial and clinical risk assessment approaches to help her make as accurate as possible an assessment of the service user and her circumstances. She accepts Helen's right to take risks in relationships and activities such as pursuing her musical interests. Margot is working to the policies and procedures of her multi-disciplinary team, will work with Helen to minimise risks to herself and to her son, and she will work in partnership with relevant colleagues and agencies. She will liaise with colleagues within her team, such as the CPN and psychiatrist, and she will work with the children and families social work colleague in another team and can make a referral to a voluntary mental health agency, MIND.

C H A P T E R   S U M M A R Y

This chapter has introduced you to assessment of risk, defined as the likelihood of something bad happening, as an integral part of social work assessment, an activity that has become more significant due to the expectations of a 'risk society' generally and a blame culture where decisions that social workers make have to be defensible.

We noted that in social work, practitioners may address the risk that some people pose to others and risks to which vulnerable people may be exposed. We explored actuarial or statistical assessment as a way of generally predicting the likelihood of risk, and clinical assessment as a way of judging risk relating to an individual based on their personal and social circumstances.

The importance of risk assessment in social work practice was highlighted by its inclusion as a key role of the National Occupational Standards for Social Work and a code in the GSCC Codes of Practice. This led to exploration of each individual's right to take risks showing that absolute safety is not always the aim in social work. There are times when positive risk taking is desirable. We considered the role of legislation, policies and procedures and risk assessment tools and their implications for a social worker's responsibility to minimise risks and protect others when appropriate. We concluded with a reminder that, as social work is increasingly a multi-agency partnership activity, it is crucial to inform relevant colleagues and agencies about the outcomes and implications of risk assessments.

FURTHER READING

Kemshall, H (2002) *Risk, social policy and welfare.* Buckingham: Open University Press.
This textbook explores risk within a social policy context and includes case examples from health, the personal social services and mental health. It examines how risk is replacing need as the key principle of welfare and state provision, with allocation of services and eligibility limits being mainly risk-based.

Kemshall, H (2008) Risk assessment and management. In Davies, M (ed) *The Blackwell companion to social work.* 3rd edition. Chapter 2.7. Oxford: Blackwell Publishing.
An easy-to-read one chapter succinct outline of risk assessment and management in social work. It explains the nature of risk and key components, and approaches to risk assessment and risk management.

Webb, S A (2006) *Social work in a risk society: Social and political perspectives.* Basingstoke: Palgrave Macmillan.
A sociological analysis focusing on social work practice and risk. It outlines the 'risk society' theoretical ideas of Beck and Giddens and draws implications for value-based practice in different settings and sectors.

Chapter 6
Children's services

This chapter will help you to meet the following National Occupational Standards:

Key Role 1: Prepare for and work with individuals, families, carers, groups and communities to assess their needs and circumstances.

- Work with individuals, families, carers, groups and communities to help them make informed decisions.
- Assess needs and options to recommend a course of action.

Key Role 2: Plan, carry out, review and evaluate social work practice with individuals, families, carers, groups and communities and other professionals.

- Address behaviour which presents a risk to individuals, families, carers, groups and communities.

Key Role 3: Support individuals to represent their needs, views and circumstances.

- Prepare for, and participate in, decision-making forums.

Key Role 4: Manage risk to individuals, families, carers, groups and communities, self and colleagues.

- Assess and manage risks to individuals, families, carers, groups and communities.

Key Role 5: Manage and be accountable, with supervision and support, for your own social work practice within your organisation.

- Work within multi-disciplinary and multi-organisational teams, networks and systems.

Key Role 6: Demonstrate professional competence in social work practice.

- Manage complex ethical issues, dilemmas and conflicts that might affect your practice.

It will also introduce you to the following academic standards as set out in the social work subject benchmark statement.

5.1.1 Social work services, service users and carers.

- The relationship between agency policies, legal requirements and professional boundaries in shaping the nature of services provided in inter-disciplinary contexts and the issues associated with working across professional boundaries and within different disciplinary groups.

5.1.2 The service delivery context.

- The issues and trends in modern public and social policy and their relationship to contemporary practice and service delivery in social work.
- The significance of legislative and legal frameworks and service delivery standards (including the nature of legal authority, the application of legislation in practice, statutory accountability and tensions between statute, policy and practice).

5.1.4 Social work theory.
- Models and methods of assessment, including factors underpinning the selection and testing of relevant information, the nature of professional judgement and the processes of risk assessment.

5.5.1 The nature of social work practice.
- The factors and processes that facilitate effective inter-disciplinary, inter-professional and inter-agency collaboration and partnership.

Problem-solving skills

5.5.2 Gathering information.
- Gather information from a wide range of sources and by a variety of methods, for a range of purposes. These methods should include electronic searches using the internet, reviews of relevant written materials, face-to-face, written and telephone contact with individuals and groups.
- Take into account differences of viewpoint in gathering information and assess the reliability and relevance of the information gathered.

5.5.3 Analysis and synthesis.
- Analyse information gathered, weighing competing evidence and modifying their viewpoint in light of new information, then relate this information to a particular task, situation or problem.

5.6 Communication skills.
- Listen actively to others, engage appropriately with the life experiences of service users, understand accurately their viewpoint and overcome personal prejudices to respond appropriately to a range of complex personal and interpersonal situations.

5.7 Skills in working with others.
- Consult actively with others, including service users, who hold relevant information or expertise.

Introduction

This chapter introduces you to assessment within children's services by putting it in the context of relevant legislation and government initiatives and developments, including requirements of statutory children and families' social workers. We will see that assessment frameworks and procedures can provide you with a structure to undertake assessments but that you will need skills, knowledge and values reviewed in previous chapters to understand the lives of individual children and their families.

Working to statutory requirements

A key piece of legislation in statutory children's services is the Children Act 1989. Implemented in 1991, it consolidated previous legislation and created a new legal framework with fundamental principles, including the following.

- The child's welfare must be paramount. A social worker must seek and take into account a child's wishes and feelings.

- Parental responsibility. A child's parents retain rights, duties and obligations, even when a child is being looked after by the local authority.

- Partnership. A social worker must involve parents and families in their work.

Sections of the Children Act 1989 give local authorities duties relevant to assessment, including the following.

- Section 17 – to safeguard and promote the welfare of *children in need*. A child is in need if he or she is unlikely to achieve reasonable standards of health or development without the provision of services, or if the child is disabled.

- Section 23 – to provide accommodation and maintain children *looked after* by the local authority;

- Section 47 – to investigate when the local authority is informed that a child is suffering, or likely to suffer, significant harm. (Child protection.)

These are examples of the children's services legal framework. While s.17 gives the local authority duties and powers relating to provision of services for children in need, social workers must assess that a child is in need using professional judgement and interpreting the somewhat limited legal definitions summarised above. S.23 gives the local authority the duty to provide accommodation and maintenance for children that it is looking after. This involves social workers assessing when a child should be in the local authority's care and what type of accommodation, including relatives, foster carers or a residential home, is most appropriate to meet the assessed needs. The duty to investigate imposed on the local authority by s.47 implies an assessment by a social worker to ascertain whether a child is being neglected or suffering some form of abuse.

Most local authorities have designated teams of social workers that are available for contact on duty, take referrals and conduct assessments. As a member of such a team you would carry out initial assessments and, depending on the outcome, you might refer the family on to another team such as those that undertake longer-term work, family support, children with disability, child protection teams, or to specialist resources such as a child and adolescence mental health team (CAMHT). The government requirement is that an *initial assessment* should be undertaken within seven days of referral and a more substantial *core assessment*, if required, within 35 days (Department of Health, 1999a).

CASE STUDY

A social worker in a duty, intake and assessment team receives a phone call from the family liaison officer (FLO) of a local primary school. The school is concerned about an eight-year-old girl who often arrives late, is dirty and dressed in worn-out clothes. She has lost weight, appears to be hungry and occasionally falls asleep in class. All this is adversely affecting her school attainment. Her mother did not respond positively when the FLO talked to her.

The social worker knows the FLO from previous contact and has a good working relationship with her. There clearly are concerns about this girl's health and development so the social worker will put the referral forward for someone in the team to undertake an initial assessment within seven days.

National developments in children's services

The Labour government elected in 1997 has been responsible for a considerable number of developments and schemes aimed at improving the quality of practice in children's services. Among these are the *Quality Protects* initiative launched in 1998 with objectives, outcomes, targets and a performance assessment framework (Department of Health, 2000). A major development to improve the quality of assessments was the *Framework for the assessment of children in need and their families* (Department of Health, et al, 2000) introduced in 2001. *Every Child Matters* initiatives first emerged in 2003; and in 2004 publications comprising the *National Service Framework for children, young people and maternity services* (Department of Health, 2004); the publication of *Common Assessment Framework* guides, forms and training materials commenced in 2005 (Children's Workforce Development Council, 2008); and the 1999 inter-agency guide *Working together to safeguard children* was updated in 2006 (Department for Education and Skills, 2006).

The framework for the assessment of children in need and their families

The framework was an attempt to shift the focus of social workers from child protection to the broader welfare needs of disadvantaged children and their families. It requires social workers to assess three *domains*:

- the child's development needs;

- parenting capacity;

- family and environmental factors.

In a diagram included in the accompanying guidance, these areas are depicted as three sides of a triangle with safeguarding and promoting the welfare of the child in the centre. The framework uses an ecological model as it requires social workers to assess the child and parents in the context of wider family and environmental factors. Local authorities have developed individual tools and their own documentation based on the framework.

In a study comparing four assessment frameworks used in the UK for different service user groups, Crisp, et al. (2007) review aspects of the *Framework for the assessment of children in need and their families*. They suggest it can provide systematised inclusion and analysis of information and encourage practitioners to draw on a range of evidence for the decisions that they make. They warn that the use of the framework as a mechanistic checklist can obscure the service users' perspectives of their needs. Important aspects in its use are:

- undertaking assessments in partnership with the child and key family members, and with their agreement (with possible exceptions when there are concerns that a child is or may be suffering significant harm);

- the identification and management of risk;

- the weight that assessors give to information;

- skilled assessors being able to articulate the reasoning for their actions;

- the essential use of supervision for those undertaking assessments;

- the need for input from a range of agencies or disciplines.

The framework will not provide you with answers to all aspects of your assessment practice; Crisp, et al. (2007, pp1073–4) state that

> ... while assessment frameworks may make explicit some expectations about the assessment process, they may also be based on an implicit assumption that persons conducting assessment already have some baseline knowledge of that process ... it would be a mistake to assume that students or new practitioners will become expert assessors simply by following the printed practice guidance.

The framework itself lists several assessment phases, *which overlap and lead into planning, action and review.* In addition to acquisition of information based on the three domains, they include:

- *exploring facts and feelings;*
- *giving meaning to the situation which distinguishes the child and family's understanding and feelings from those of the professionals;*
- *reaching an understanding of what is happening, problems, strengths and difficulties, and the impact on the child (with the family wherever possible);*
- *drawing up an analysis of the needs of the child and parenting capacity within their family and community context as a basis for formulating a plan*
(Department of Health, et al., 2000, p29).

The above shows that, while the material provides a *framework* for assessment, your professional social work skills, knowledge and underpinning values are integral to your involvement with service users.

CASE STUDY

Tamsin's family assessment

Tamsin, a social worker in a children and families long-term team, has had a referral from the intake team, for a core child in need (CHIN) assessment. There was a previous CHIN referral last year but, following assessment, the family were referred to a local family centre.

The family consists of Sally (28), who has a ten-year-old son Liam from a previous relationship, and has been living with Jack (29) on and off for the past four years. They have a two-year-old daughter Becky from their relationship. The main concern is Liam, whose school attendance is very poor and, when he is there, he is said to be disruptive

→

CASE STUDY *continued*

and aggressive. He is in serious risk of exclusion. He stays out late and recently was out all night. The parents find him disobedient and Sally says he is 'beyond control'. There is some suggestion that Liam has been seen smoking crack cocaine.

Sally and Jack have a turbulent relationship and a history of substance misuse. Jack left home recently after hitting Sally and breaking her arm following a heated argument. He has been unemployed recently and there are considerable rent arrears. The house is in a poor state of repair and cleanliness.

Addressing the first domain of the framework, Tamsin will:

* *assess Liam's physical, cognitive and emotional developmental needs;*
* *make contact with other professionals such as the school and GP with the family's consent;*
* *discuss with Liam his relationships at home, at school and with local friends;*
* *note how he engages with her, his feelings about his current circumstances and his understanding of safety regarding using drugs;*
* *take into account his wishes about his immediate and longer-term future.*

In assessing parenting capacity, Tamsin will endeavour to see Sally and Jack, and discuss areas including:

* *their basic care of the children and how they ensure their safety;*
* *their guidance of the children, setting boundaries and how consistent they are in their discipline;*
* *their own relationship and misuse of drugs;*
* *a typical day with the children and any incidents at home or school that gave them cause for concern regarding Liam;*
* *their parenting of Becky;*
* *what family life means to them, whether they encourage Liam with his schooling and how they engage in play and other activities with their children.*

To assess family and environmental factors, Tamsin will enquire about:

* *Sally and Jack's backgrounds, possibly using a genogram as a tool to discuss their family histories;*
* *any extended family links and other possible sources of support;*
* *their situation as regards finances, accommodation, employment and income;*
* *their involvement in the community, possibly using an eco map as a tool to explore their support systems.*

Millar and Corby (2006) conducted a study of the use of the framework based on interviews with service users and social workers. They found that assessments based on the framework *can result in outcomes that service users find helpful.* However, there was some evidence that for service users to find the process a 'therapeutic' encounter

> *the skill and approach of the social worker could make a significant difference. The ability to create a positive atmosphere, reducing tension and providing 'space' was helpful* ...

(p895)

This was despite suggestions that the associated form filling is a time-consuming obstacle for social workers to engage helpfully with people and that the framework might be seen to encapsulate an ethos of management and scrutiny.

The framework's practice guidance has helpful theoretical underpinning and includes a chapter on assessing black children in need and their families (Dutt and Phillips, 2000). Bernard and Gupta (2008, p486) point out that *the fear of being seen as racist, combined with cultural stereotypes, can lead to a failure to make judgements and intervene appropriately regarding practices that are clearly harmful.* In a review of the literature on African children's involvement in the child protection system, they argue that:

> *The complex social circumstances experienced by many African families pose challenges for parents and children, as well as professionals working to safeguard and promote children's welfare. The* Framework for the Assessment of Children in Need and their Families *(Department of Health, 2000) based on the ecological approach places a requirement on workers to consider families' histories and social circumstances and the literature on anti-oppressive practice stresses the importance of consideration being paid to power relationships.*

There may be particular issues in seeking and taking into account black children's wishes and feelings in assessment. Graham (2007) reviews the influence of a new sociology of childhood generally, relating it specifically to black children, and advocates for participatory approaches to incorporate new initiatives in working with black children. Bernard (2002, p249) explores the process of 'telling' and the difficulties of voicing experiences for some black children, pointing out that

> *to be able to hear what black children are telling us, and perhaps more importantly, paying attention to the silences surrounding what they are not telling us is a crucial component of risk assessment.*

Parents and families

Since the legislation states that the child's welfare must be paramount, there is a danger that social workers, in spite of the framework's three domains, focus too narrowly on the child they are assessing. Wilson, et al. (2008, p466) highlight the difficult dilemma of working with children *and* families, not children *or* families. They point out that although some inquiries into the deaths of children have found that social workers had difficulty *'holding the child in mind' and not having their attention diverted to the child's parent/carers,* a solution is not

> to focus simply on the child and overlook other family members. All children are located in social systems and promoting their best interests involves working with their social networks as well as with them. Children come to the attention of social workers because of deprived, disadvantaged, dysfunctional or abusive family circumstances and often their parents have grown up in similar situations.

In their research into how mothers cope with childcare and associated problems when they do not gain access to social services support, Sheppard and Grohn (2003) advocate a greater focus on and support for mothers. They suggest mothers are often lost in the social work interpretation of the *welfare of the child is paramount,* which they may understand as *I don't matter much as a person in my own right.* Sheppard and Grohn (2003) question how can you best look after the welfare of the child unless you pay attention to their mother? They point out that mothers are generally the primary carers and overwhelmingly so with applicants to and recipients of children's services. Quite often the father is not in the picture, a large majority of families having been the subject of breakdown or never having had the father living with them.

RESEARCH SUMMARY

Farnfield (2008) locates parenting within an ecological framework to propose a theoretical model for its comprehensive assessment. The model is rooted in attachment theory and evolutionary psychology, with an overarching use of systemic thinking. He defines a care-giving environment separating core dimensions that are fundamental to parenting behaviour (an intrinsic part of the behaviour of all parents) from individual modifiers that affect parenting ability. The seven dimensions considered are:

Core dimensions intrinsic to parenting

Childhood attachment system

1. *The parent's state of mind regarding their own childhood attachments.*
2. *The parent's degree of resolution regarding loss and trauma.*

+

The spousal/pair bonding system

3. *The state of the marriage/adult sexual partnership.*

+

The affiliative/wider support system

4. *Family, friends and community resources.*

+

The care-giving system

5. *The meaning of the child to the parent.*
6. **Modifiers**
    Type 1. Intra- or interpersonal (including mental and physical health, disabilities, substance misuse, other behaviour and family factors).

→

Type 2. Cultural/socio-economic (including cultural norms, how a particular people have survived danger over time, subcultural strategies).

*7. **Integration** intrapersonal neurological information processing, which enables the human mind to note discrepancies between different types and sources of information.*

*8. **The child***

He suggests relevant assessment procedures and tools (e.g. Adult Attachment Inventory).

The *Every Child Matters* agenda

A significant impetus for change in the last few years was the tragic death in February 2000 of eight-year-old Victoria Climbié from the Ivory Coast at the hands of her aunt and her aunt's partner following abuse and some 128 injuries, despite opportunities to remove her from their care during contact with local authority social services departments, hospitals, the police and the National Society for the Prevention of Cruelty to Children (NSPCC).

Lord Laming was asked to undertake an inquiry (Laming, 2003) and its wide-ranging findings and recommendations have implications for assessment. An important theme was the lack of communication and sharing of information between different agencies so that no one agency had the full picture of what was happening. There were also racial considerations. Black carers killed a black child and the social worker and police officer most closely involved were black. Bernard and Gupta (2008, pp485–6) refer to stereotypical racist assumptions, for example:

> *Victoria standing to attention, being frightened, and, on occasions, wetting herself when her aunt visited her in hospital were assumed to be a reflection of the way African children show respect to their elders and was therefore not deemed an issue for concern; a detailed assessment of her individual needs and relationships was never undertaken.*

The government accepted the Laming recommendations and as a response published the Green Paper *Every Child Matters* (Department of Education and Skills, 2003), putting forward proposals for effective protection of children through new partnerships, cross-sector workforce reform and more accountability. Legislation from these proposals came into force with the Children Act 2004, which did not replace the Children Act 1989, but added requirements about the organisation of children's services. A major one was the restructuring of local authority directorates through the requirement that there must be a Director of Children's Services. Most local authorities created new departments of Children, Families and Education, separate from departments dealing with adults and community services.

This reflected the central government restructuring of responsibility in 2003 with the creation of a Minister of State for Children, Young People and Families post within the then Department for Education and Skills. The change separated children services from social care services for older people, disabled people and those with mental health problems, responsibility for which remained with the Department of Health. In June 2007 this trend was taken further, with the children's minister becoming part of a newly created Department for Children, Schools and Families.

This, for some controversial, split is further mirrored in other bodies such as the Children's Workforce Development Council (CWDC) becoming a separate body from Skills for Care in 2006, with responsibility for information sharing, the Common Assessment Framework, the 'lead professional' concept in integrated support, and multi-agency working. In 2007 the Association of Directors of Social Services (ADSS) and Confed (the corresponding education body) reorganised in England into the Association of Directors of Children's Services (ADCS) and the Association of Directors of Adult Services (ADAS); and Ofsted, the body responsible for inspections of schools, took over from the then Commission for Social Care Inspection (CSCI) the regulation and inspection of all services for children, young people, families and education.

Central and local government changes reflect policy that puts emphasis on the well-being of all children and young people from birth to age 19. *Every Child Matters* (Department of Education and Skills, 2003) outlines the government aim for every child, whatever their background or their circumstances, to have the support they need to:

- be healthy;
- stay safe;
- enjoy and achieve;
- make a positive contribution;
- achieve economic well-being.

These laudable but very general five outcomes may have the result that child protection, such an important part of social workers' involvement with children and families, is not as prominent a concern for children's services as a whole.

In reviewing the role of child and family social work in the light of recent policy developments, Spratt (2009, p436) considers that:

> *In relocating the risks with regard to children away from narrow concerns to prevent the occurrence or reoccurrence of abuse, and within a more sophisticated appreciation of how the experience of present problems may be associated with poor outcomes across a number of domains in later life, the social policy function of social workers (which grew out of and was sustained by concerns on the part of the public to manage the phenomenon of child abuse) becomes subsumed within new priorities to strategically invest in children and families.*

On the other hand, statutory social workers cannot meet all the needs of children and families, and local authorities inevitably have eligibility thresholds. As mentioned in Chapter 1, one aspect of undertaking an assessment involves you in assessing eligibility for services and level of need. Having completed an initial assessment, you will be responsible for telling the family whether or not the local authority can offer services. If a family does not meet the eligibility criteria you should explain reasons for this to them, normally in writing, and you probably will suggest alternative sources of help.

RESEARCH SUMMARY

Sheppard (2009) conducted a study of families who were unsuccessful applicants for children's social services in a city in southern England due to the high thresholds used in assessing need. One hundred and two women were interviewed to investigate which coping strategies following the unsuccessful applications were most effective in securing positive outcomes. Sixty-nine were further interviewed in a six-month follow-up. Using ideas from coping theory, Sheppard hypothesised that outcomes would vary according to the mother's coping strategy. Mothers might seek to problem solve the situation through direct action, seek social support, engage in restraint, reinterpretation and growth, turn to religion and use acceptance, denial and disengagement strategies. Mothers are generally the primary carers, more so with applicants to children's services. Coping theory allows the participant to comment on the role of others, including the father, in helping to cope.

Coping through direct action, restraint, reinterpretation and growth, and turning to religion were not found to be significant.

Seeking social support showed an increase in child development (p < 0.046) and child and parenting (p < 0.043) measures. The reduction in depression symptoms through social support fell just below significance.

Avoidance strategies such as denial and disengagement produced a statistical significant increase in depression symptoms (p < 0.003).

There are limitations to this study such as its size, being carried out in one predominantly white area and being based on mothers' self-reports. However, it provides some evidence to show that the act of seeking social support (as opposed to its enactment) can be important for improved outcomes. This is a group of service users for whom the social worker undertaking the assessment might consider referral to children's centres or other similar agencies. If a mother is disengaging because she has 'given up', help to enable her to engage better with parenting and child development issues could be of considerable importance.

Common Assessment Framework

The government is developing a number of measures concerning the well-being of children, young people and families within the *Every Child Matters* agenda, with publications such as *Youth Matters* (2005), *Youth Matters – Next steps* (2006), *Care Matters: Transforming the lives of children and young people* (2006) and *Every Parent Matters* (Department for Education and Skills, 2007) making proposals and setting expectations of how the five outcomes apply to young people and children in care, and how they can be promoted by parents. The Child Care Act 2006 is the first-ever exclusively concerned with early years childcare provision. It promotes the Every Child

Matters principles for pre-school children and assumes involvement by local authorities and the private and voluntary sectors. The Green Paper *Care Matters* led to the Children and Young Persons Act 2008, which extends the statutory framework for children in care to ensure they receive quality care, stability of placements and improve their educational experience and attainment. Local authorities will appoint Independent Reviewing Officers.

Within these government objectives, a tool to promote assessment, information sharing and earlier intervention from child welfare practitioners is the *Common Assessment Framework* (CAF). Pithouse, et al. (2009, p599) describe it as *an electronic system for assessing children and sharing information between child care professionals.* They review its introduction and pilot trials and point out that

> In the course of implementation, policy aims have become submerged in day-to-day practice and that, analytically, there are differences between the 'CAF of policy' and the 'CAF of practice'; in brief ... there are all manner of common assessment designs operating in the world of practice.

The CAF documentation (Children's Workforce Development Council, 2009) includes a 'windscreen' curved shaped diagram illustrating a continuum of needs and services subdivided from left to right into four levels.

- The first level involves *universal services for all children and young people* for those *with no identified additional needs.*

- The second level is *targeted support by a single practitioner* (from an agency such as a school) for *children with additional needs.*

- The third level involves *targeted support* provided as *integrated support* by a *lead professional* with an intervention plan arising from a CAF assessment for *children with additional needs.*

- The fourth level is *integrated support from statutory or specialist services* for a small proportion of *children with complex needs* who are part of the *broader group of children with additional needs* and meet the threshold for statutory involvement. For instance, social workers would undertake s.17 *child in need* and s.47 *child protection* assessments using the *Framework for the assessment of children in need and their families.*

In spite of this comprehensive, and perhaps over-optimistic, framework with electronic assessment forms, CAF is a voluntary arrangement aiming to promote practitioners, children, young people, parents and carers to share information about needs and cooperate to meet them. Pithouse, et al. (2009, p600) state that

> it is not a suitable tool for immediate and referable concerns about child protection, nor is it intended to replace specialist and statutory assessments.

It appears that in some areas the CAF is being used as a referral form, particularly by sectors such as detached workers, voluntary agencies and community projects previously without an assessment remit.

Integrated Children's System

The Integrated Children's System (ICS) is a government initiative providing a framework for electronic management of information involved in social workers' assessment, planning, intervention and review. In an evaluation of four pilot sites, Shaw, et al. (2009, p614) say of ICS:

> It is intended to apply to all children in need in England and Wales – about 370,000 at any one time – and not only 'looked after' children (about 60,000) or those on nationally required and locally maintained 'child protection registers' (about 26,000). The ICS is not a marginal development, but is intended to lie at the heart of statutory child-care practice in England and Wales.

The ICS includes data requirements and 'exemplar' forms to be used by local authorities in setting up computer systems that can be home-grown or developed by commercial suppliers. This in itself is a development problem as the system is not uniform throughout the country.

There has been much criticism from social workers about the ICS. The Social Work Task Force in 2009 (see further comments about it below) was told that social workers feel they do not have enough time to devote directly to the people they want to help as they are tied up in bureaucracy. Social workers reported that compliance with the ICS makes record keeping a burdensome process and drives a model of practice that can be at odds with professional judgement. The ICS is intended to manage large amounts of data, including information about referrals, the service user child and family, details of other professionals, and assessment as a child in need, looked after, or in need of protection. The data are only as reliable as the actual information that social workers input and the evaluation found considerable levels of human error.

RESEARCH SUMMARY

As part of their evaluation of four ICS pilot sites in England and Wales, Shaw et al. (2009) included focus groups to seek the views of social workers about their experiences using ICS. While in principle welcoming the idea of a common computerised system with potential for communication across agencies, they did not think this was the outcome in practice. They experienced ICS as time consuming and the exemplars prescriptive, repetitive and fragmented.

The researches asked social workers to estimate the time they spent between six activities by the type of exemplar. These are shown in the table below.

Mean time in hours spent on six activities by assessment type							
Assessment type	Consultation with other agencies	Consultation within department	Direct contact with child/family	Informal network	Entering data	Other activities	N*
Initial assessment	1.65	0.79	2.5	0.02	2.56	2.83	22
Core assessment	12.01	4.2	10.9	0.39	8.47	13.14	19
Child plan	6.49	1.94	6.14	0.15	3.83	9.27	13
Review	4.42	1.50	15.03	0.26	2.91	12.41	12
Total	6.09	2.13	7.91	0.20	4.58	8.81	66

N = Number of social workers providing the time estimatation.

→

Further government developments

Some of the latest developments in social work were triggered by the death of 17-month-old baby P, later identified as Peter Connelly, in August 2008. He was on the child protection register of Haringey Council (criticised over the death of Victoria Climbié in 2000) for eight months while he was abused to the extent of suffering 50 injuries. Lord Laming was asked to prepare a report on safeguarding arrangements, resulting in *The protection of children in England: A progress report* (Laming, 2009). The government also set up a Social Work Task Force to look at the reform of the social work system. In its first report in May 2009 the Task Force made recommendations about ICS, which the government accepted. They involved relaxing specification requirements, and introducing increased flexibility and evaluation tools. It its final report (November 2009, p10) the Task Force recommended that

> DCSF and local authorities should continue to improve the Integrated Children's System (ICS), by translating national specifications into tangible improvements to local systems, making ICS more straightforward and effective for frontline social workers in children's services.

Coordinated assessment

The government aims to integrate services for children and young people with a variety of agencies involved in sharing information. A tool to achieve this is the ContactPoint (Department for Children, Schools and Families, 2009) database that has been introduced to hold basic details about every child in England, whether an assessment has been carried out, although not the assessment information, and whether anyone is working with the child or young person. This will be available to all relevant workers.

The CAF is the tool to be used at an early stage to assess needs, gather and record information and decide on action. Practitioners across all agencies will be expected to do this in a coordinated way. It is intended that an electronic CAF system will allow sharing of this information.

In the case of children with complex needs, social workers will be involved in assessing whether they are or may be children in need as defined by legislation, including those who have suffered neglect or abuse or are looked after, using the *Framework for the assessment of children in need and their families*, systematically recording information about the child and family. The ICS is the tool for working with these children and managing detailed information requirements. Any CAF information will be incorporated into the assessment section of ICS. Basic ICS information, though not the case details, about involvement and the practitioner to contact will be uploaded to Con-tactPoint.

Assessment of child maltreatment

ACTIVITY **6.1**

Write down your honest personal responses to the points below:

- *What are your feelings about physical, sexual and emotional abuse and neglect of children?*
- *What is the personal impact on you when you consider neglect and abuse?*
- *If you are a student, how do you think you will cope, and if you are a qualified social worker, how do you cope in interaction with families when investigating whether a child is suffering, or is likely to suffer, significant harm?*
- *What difficult questions might you have to ask?*
- *What distressing information might you be given?*

Comment

This activity may have elicited punitive and retaliatory thoughts, anger, abhorrence, fear, sadness, sympathy, and many more possibly mixed feelings. One of the most difficult areas of work you will face when undertaking assessments is looking into the possibility that child neglect or abuse is taking place. You will be using communica-tion, observation and investigative skills. You will need an understanding of child abuse and neglect and knowledge of human development and behaviour. You will face ethical dilemmas and have to work to professional values. You will be assessing the risk that parents or others pose to a child and how vulnerable a child is to sig-nificant harm. You will be communicating and sharing information with other professionals who also face the complex task of judging the extent of the concerns. Your involvement will have considerable impact on you as a person.

Assessment will also have a significant effect on the child and family concerned. Hol-land (2004) argues that the seemingly neutral process of carrying out assessments should always be expected to have an impact on the participants, because the very act of being asked questions and explaining our situation to others is likely to make us reflect and come to understand our situation in a new light.

CASE STUDY

Anna has contacted the local authority children's services because she is worried that her husband, Mike, often wakes up their nine-year-old daughter Zoë around 11pm to say goodnight, whispers to her and kisses her on her face, neck and arms for at least 30

→

minutes. He sometimes shuts the door. Anna's mother visited recently, stayed overnight and witnessed this. Anna and Mike have three children – Zoë (9), Matthew (7) and Samantha (5) – but it is only with Zoë that Mike behaves in this way. Anna and Mike's relationship is near breakdown and they are discussing separation and divorce. They do not sleep together. A few days ago Anna checked on Zoë near midnight because Mike had been there so long and he was in bed with her.

Olivia, a social worker from the child protection team, will visit to undertake a detailed assessment and her aim will initially be to interview Zoë, Anna and Mike separately.

Olivia will use sensitive and age-appropriate communication skills to engage with Zoë. Interaction will be through talking and listening carefully to her, but may also include drawing, the use of dolls to represent people, buttons to represent relationships, or other similar techniques. Issues to explore include:

- *Her understanding of sexuality and her body.*

- *Whether she considers her father's behaviour wrong or something to be accepted from him.*

- *Whether she thinks a lot about what happens between them. Has she any thought triggers or flashbacks?*

- *How she sleeps. Has she any nightmares?*

- *The relationship she has with her father in general.*

- *Her relationship with her mother and siblings.*

- *How she is doing at school.*

When interviewing Anna, Olivia will be aware of the views of Erooga and Print (2001, p310), who state that:

> *Non-abusing parents…should have the motivation, capacity and ability to under-stand and respond to the psychological and emotional needs of a child who has ex-perienced abuse. In addition, they must understand the ways in which the abuser has coerced the child into compliance, often referred to as 'grooming methods'.*

Olivia will take this knowledge into consideration while showing empathy but conduct-ing an objective investigation. Erooga and Print (2001, pp311–12) also include among factors to consider when assessing a mother's capacity to protect and support a child who might be sexually abused:

- *position regarding responsibility and blame;*

- *perceived options;*

- *cooperation with statutory agencies;*

- *relationship history;*

- *history of sexual abuse.*

→

In a non-judgemental way, Olivia will want to obtain factual details from Mike about the nature of his behaviour, assess the risk of the behaviour continuing, the stage of his relationship with Anna and whether they will be separating. If she assesses that abuse is taking place, she may refer the matter to the police.

In serious cases there may not be an initial assessment. In accordance with *Working Together* guidelines (Department for Education and Skills, 2006) there will probably be a strategic meeting involving police, health, education and other professionals to decide whether to take urgent action such as removing a child to a place of safety, and plan to undertake a core assessment to investigate whether a child is suffering, or likely to suffer, significant harm. A s.47 enquiry may lead to a child protection conference, within 15 days of the strategy discussion, involving all relevant professionals and the family.

In a study of referral practice in cases of child neglect in the Republic of Ireland Horwath (2007) noted that assessment frameworks and tools usually focus on *technical–rational activity* associated with assessing children and families in their environment. Her findings indicated that assessment practice is as much a *practice–moral activity* as a technical–rational one. As the author states, *it is both a head and heart activity.* Factors influencing assessment included the professional's own interpretation of what is neglect; the extent to which they used a 'gut-reaction' or an evidence base; their interpretation of professional roles in relation to assessing and referring and the views of their colleagues and team manager; professionals' perceptions of social work services and benefits of a referral; and their own personal feelings such as fear, guilt, over-empathy and anxiety about the response of the community. Horwath (2007) suggests that these factors constitute a *practitioner domain* missing from assessment frameworks.

C H A P T E R   S U M M A R Y

In considering assessment within children's services we started by putting it in the context of key legislation and statutory organisation and requirements. From a review of various government initiatives and developments we highlighted the *Framework for the assessment of children in need and their families.* We noted the dangers of using it mechanistically and saw the need for involving service users, multi-agency input, and for assessment skills, judgement and a professional approach, because while gathering factual information you will also be dealing with people's feelings. Other considerations included the need for cultural awareness, avoiding stereotypes, and focusing on the family as well as the child, since children are located within family and social systems. We saw that the assessment of parenting is important.

The chapter outlined the *Every Child Matters* agenda and government policy aimed at the well-being of all children, with a separation of children and adult services at central and local government. While accepting the limits of statutory social workers' involvement, we considered eligibility thresholds. The chapter introduced you to the Common Assessment Framework (CAF), addressing a continuum of needs and services from universal services for all children and young people to specialist statutory services for a small proportion of children with complex needs. We noted that, as a voluntary arrangement, CAF has had an uneven take-up. The chapter also introduced you to the Integrated Children's System (ICS), a framework for electronic management of information for all children in need across agencies. As each local authority adapts the scheme to its local systems, there is criticism that ICS is time consuming, repetitive and fragmented, although the Social Work Task Force has made recommendations for improvements. We noted the introduction of the ContactPoint database to share information among all agencies involved in children's services, with its aim to have data on every child in England. Within this coordination, CAF can be used for assessing needs at an early stage and social workers are involved in a statutory response to children with complex needs, assessing them using the *Framework for the assessment of children in need and their families* with ICS as the tool for working with these children and managing information.

The chapter concluded with an exploration of assessment in child maltreatment and the personal impact it may have on you and on the child and family concerned. We saw that assessment frameworks tend to imply a *technical–rational* activity whereas in the area of child protection assessment will engage you in *practice–moral* activity involving both head and heart.

FURTHER READING

Horwath J (2001) *The child's world: Assessing children in need.* London: Jessica Kingsley Publishers. This book was commissioned by the Department of Health to outline developments relating to the *Framework for the assessment of children in need and their families.* Although some years old now, it includes fundamental underpinning theory about assessment, the developmental needs of children and parenting.

Holland, S (2004) *Child and family assessment in social work practice.* London: Sage.
This is a useful source of theory and how it can be integrated with practice. It explores different approaches to assessment and goes on to apply the ideas to children, their parents and the relationship between the assessors and the assessed.

O'Loughlin, M and O'Loughlin, S (2008) *Social work with children and families.* Exeter: Learning Matters.
A broader introduction to multi-agency work, skills, knowledge and values. It includes the legislation framework and a chapter on social work with children with disabilities and their families, an area not covered in the above chapter.

WEBSITES

www.dcsf.gov.uk/
The Department for Children, Schools and Families (DCSF) is the Government department with responsibility for children's services.

www.dcsf.gov.uk/everychildmatters/
Within the DCSF website, the Every Child Matters programme website sets out Government's initiatives and plans for reforms.

www.dh.gov.uk/en/Healthcare/Children/index.htm
The Department of Health retains responsibility for child health promotion.

www.11million.org.uk/
The Children's Commissioner for England website's name highlights that there are 11 million children and young people in England that have the right to a voice.

www.sccyp.org.uk/
www.childcomwales.org.uk/
www.niccy.org/
The offices of Children Commissioners for Scotland, Wales and Northern Ireland have their own websites.

www.direct.gov.uk/en/Parents/index.htm
www.direct.gov.uk/en/YoungPeople/index.htm
The Government's information website Directgov has sections about parents and young people.

Chapter 7
Adult services and community care

A C H I E V I N G   A   S O C I A L   W O R K   D E G R E E

This chapter will help you to meet the following National Occupational Standards:

Key Role 1: Prepare for and work with individuals, families, carers, groups and communities to assess their needs and circumstances.
- Work with individuals, families, carers, groups and communities to help them make informed decisions.
- Assess needs and options to recommend a course of action.

Key Role 2: Plan, carry out, review and evaluate social work practice with individuals, families, carers, groups and communities and other professionals.
- Address behaviour which presents a risk to individuals, families, carers, groups and communities.

Key Role 3: Support individuals to represent their needs, views and circumstances.
- Prepare for and participate in decision-making forums.

Key Role 4: Manage risk to individuals, families, carers, groups and communities, self and colleagues.
- Assess and manage risks to individuals, families, carers, groups and communities.

Key Role 5: Manage and be accountable, with supervision and support, for your own social work practice within your organisation.
- Work within multi-disciplinary and multi-organisational teams, networks and systems.

Key Role 6: Demonstrate professional competence in social work practice.
- Manage complex ethical issues, dilemmas and conflicts that might affect your practice.

It will also introduce you to the following academic standards as set out in the social work subject benchmark statement.

5.1.1 Social work services, service users and carers.
- The relationship between agency policies, legal requirements and professional boundaries in shaping the nature of services provided in inter-disciplinary contexts and the issues associated with working across professional boundaries and within different disciplinary groups.

5.1.2 The service delivery context.
- The issues and trends in modern public and social policy and their relationship to contemporary practice and service delivery in social work.
- The significance of legislative and legal frameworks and service delivery standards (including the nature of legal authority, the application of legislation in practice, statutory accountability and tensions between statute, policy and practice).

5.1.4 Social work theory.
- Models and methods of assessment, including factors underpinning the selection and testing of relevant information, the nature of professional judgement and the processes of risk assessment.

5.1.5 The nature of social work practice.
- The factors and processes that facilitate effective inter-disciplinary, inter-professional and inter-agency collaboration and partnership.

Problem-solving skills.

5.5.2 Gathering information.
- Gather information from a wide range of sources and by a variety of methods, for a range of purposes. These methods should include electronic searches using the internet, reviews of relevant written materials, face-to-face, written and telephone contact with individuals and groups.
- Take into account differences of viewpoint in gathering information and assess the reliability and relevance of the information gathered.

5.5.3 Analysis and synthesis.
- Analyse information gathered, weighing competing evidence and modifying their viewpoint in light of new information, then relate this information to a particular task, situation or problem.

5.6 Communication Skills.
- Listen actively to others, engage appropriately with the life experiences of service users, understand accurately their viewpoint and overcome personal prejudices to respond appropriately to a range of complex personal and interpersonal situations.

5.7 Skills in working with others.
- Consult actively with others, including service users, who hold relevant information or expertise.

Introduction

In this chapter we will consider assessment within adult services and community care, starting with the legislative context and going on to review government initiatives and developments, including the current personalisation agenda, relating to this area of statutory social work. We will focus specifically on work with older persons and adults with learning and physical disabilities, although some of what this chapter outlines applies to a number of other service user groups of people 18 years old and over that include those with HIV and Aids, deaf and hearing-impaired people, persons involved in substance misuse and asylum seekers.

Working to statutory requirements

The National Health Service (NHS) and Community Care Act 1990 places a duty on local authorities to assess a person's need for community care services and decide whether to provide them.

Section 47 (1) states:

> ... *where it appears to a local authority that any person for whom they may provide or arrange for the provision of community care services may be in need of any such services, the authority –*

(a) shall carry out an assessment of his needs for those services; and

(b) having regard to the results of the assessment, shall decide whether his needs call for the provision by them of such services.

(Office of Public Sector Information, 1990)

Previous legislation is still in force giving local authorities powers to provide services. The National Assistance Act 1948, which abolished the Poor Law, for instance, governs provision of accommodation and other welfare services.

Care management

It was the NHS and Community Care Act 1990 that gave local authority *care managers* the role of assessment. Due to government concerns about the increase of residential care funded by benefit payments, Sir Roy Griffiths, deputy chairman of Sainsbury's supermarket, was asked to examine the system of community care. In his 1988 report *Community care: Agenda for action* Griffiths suggested a *care management* system where councils would assess needs and design *packages of care* purchased from a *mixed economy* of private, voluntary and statutory providers. The ensuing government 1989 White Paper *Caring for People: Community care in the next decade and beyond* led to the 1990 Act. This created a *purchaser–provider split* and confirmed a move away from institutional and residential care. Local authority *care managers* became responsible for assessing, planning, purchasing, monitoring and reviewing care packages.

CASE STUDY

Edith and Frank

Richard, a care manager, has assessed Edith (79), referred by her GP (see p81). Her mobility is restricted and she has been diagnosed as having dementia. Her husband Frank (80) is not used to household tasks and has to increasingly care for Edith.

Having received the referral, Richard is acting on the local authority's duty imposed by the NHS and Community Care Act 1990 s.47 (1) (a) to carry out an assessment of Edith's needs for services. Richard visits Edith and Frank and talks to them about their circumstances and what would help them cope better. He also observes them interacting, noting for instance Edith's confusion when making a cup of tea, which she offers, and Frank taking over for her. Richard informs Frank that, as a carer, he is also entitled to an assessment.

Following the 1990 Act s.47 (1) (b), Richard decides that Edith's needs call for the provision of services and discusses a care package that involves carers from a private agency coming in twice a day to undertake Edith's personal care, such as helping her to get up and go to bed, dress and wash; and a private contractor delivering frozen meals that can be heated to eat at a time of their choice. A microwave and freezer are provided on free loan. In addition, Richard investigates the possibility of Edith and Frank attending a local older persons day centre run by a voluntary organisation to give them a break once or twice a week.

→

Due to the level of their savings, they are assessed as having to make a financial contribution towards this package. When the plans are in place, Richard will monitor and review their effectiveness.

ACTIVITY **7.1**

If you are studying towards a social work qualification, would you consider working within adult services and community care?
In your opinion, are social work skills needed to work with older people and other adult service users?
What skills and knowledge do you think you will need?

Comment

As a care manager you will need skills in or at least a basic understanding of financial assessments, administering budgets, commissioning services, contracting with providers and purchasing care packages, as well as assessing needs within a supportive relationship. Local authorities have accepted qualifications such as nursing and occupational therapy, as well as social work, for care managers, so a debate in recent years has been whether care managers are social workers.

A report by the Training Organisation for Personal Social Services (Topss) England (now Skills for Care) Workforce Intelligence Unit stated:

> *Among older social workers in particular, the move to care management is a source of dissatisfaction, because it reduces the amount of direct contact with service users and hence opportunities to 'make a difference', while at the same time increasing bureaucracy and procedures. Some care managers feel they have lost some of their social work skills, and are divorced from the people they serve.*

> (Eborall, 2003, p7)

For many this area of work is a fulfilling one. Social workers and care managers within community care services are increasingly engaged in multi-agency joint assessments, typically with health professionals. They may be seconded to an NHS Trust and/or be part of multi-disciplinary integrated teams.

National developments in adult services and community care

In 1998 the Department of Health launched a rolling programme of *National Service Frameworks* (NSFs) for a number of areas including cancer, mental health, coronary heart disease, diabetes and older people, to set national standards, put in place strategies, raise quality and reduce variations in services.

The NSF for Older People was published in 2001 (Department of Health, 2001a). In their study comparing four assessment frameworks, Crisp, et al. (2007) include the framework for older people and state (pp1066–7) that it seeks

> *to identify persons who are perceived to be vulnerable so that measures can be taken to reduce or avoid potential for significant harm, in respect of older persons, the role of assessments is also to promote independence where possible by seeking to prevent deterioration and manage crises.*

The NSF promotes a person-centred approach with an expectation that the needs of the person being assessed will be paramount and not lost among the needs of other family members. It sets out eight standards, the first of which is *Rooting out age discrimination*, addressing diversity and disadvantage. It highlights the needs of service users for whom English is not their first language in relation to provision of information.

Providing *culturally competent* care includes taking into account individuals' religious, cultural and linguistic needs. Minhas, et al. (2002, p12) reject a 'colour blind approach', which

> *Implies that all service users have the same needs and should therefore be treated the same. This approach views diverse or different needs negatively and expects Black and minority ethnic service users to 'fit-in' with Eurocentric services.*

The NSF sets out requirements for partnership working. A single assessment process (SAP) for health and social care is a key element of standard 2 (person-centred care). The government published assessment tools and other guidance to support implementation of the SAP by 2004 (Department of Health, 2002a). While containing helpful material relevant to various aspects of assessment, a criticism is that they are too long a list of tick-box items.

The SAP has assessment documents that local social care and health authorities adapt into their own common assessment tools, including availability to run on a desktop, laptop or pocket PC. Some of these allow for more qualitative answers rather than a mainly tick-box approach. The Department of Health accredits private companies to provide personal information, recording and measurement systems (FACE, 2009) that can be more outcomes-focused. The types of assessment included in SAP documents are listed in Table 7.1.

When someone is referred or makes personal contact, a background or *contact assessment* is carried out to collect basic information. The legal duty to carry out an assessment *where it appears to a local authority* that a person may be in need of services, allows councils to undertake this initial screening before deciding to assess further. There is a danger that this stage may not be specific enough and councils might not go on to assess someone who has a need of services.

Table 7.1

Type of assessment	Information gathered	Who is involved
Contact assessment	Basic personal and background information. Nature of presenting problem.	May be undertaken on the telephone, or service users complete the form themselves.
Overview assessment	Broad outline of circumstances. May help identify areas where more detailed assessment is needed.	Normally a single practitioner.
Specialist (in-depth) assessment	Specific needs. Health condition(s) and/or social care need(s).	May involve physiotherapist, nurse or occupational therapist.
Comprehensive assessment	Sum total of information gathered through contact, overview and/or specialist assessments. All or most of the SAP areas, including assessment of rehabilitation potential.	Range of professionals or specialist teams, including medical assessments. Named care coordinator.
Risk assessment	Personal safety. Which risks are worth taking and which should be reduced, managed or removed.	Care coordinator, e.g. using *FACE Risk Profile Tool*.
Carer's needs assessment	Needs and circumstances of an individual carer. Ability to continue caring. Support that may be provided.	Care coordinator. May involve an element of self-assessment.

If needs or risks that require further investigation are identified, an *overview assessment* may be carried out, which can lead on to a more in-depth *specialist assessment*. Other documents available within the SAP are *comprehensive, risk and carer's needs assessments*.

CASE STUDY

A GP referred Mrs Benson (79) for an assessment after she had a fall. The GP noted that she was physically frail and finding it increasingly difficult to cope on her own. If a SAP contact assessment of Mrs Benson's needs and risks showed that her situation requires further investigation, an overview assessment would be conducted based on her medical and social history. In some areas a health practitioner from a 'rapid response' team may undertake this. Some councils may also involve a care manager.

A health assessment would include Mrs Benson's:

- *physical health;*
- *mobility;*
- *personal care, continence, daily routines;*
- *any falls and accidents;*
- *sleep patterns;*
- *ability to bath, shower, use the toilet;*
- *sight, hearing and communication;*
- *ability to cook, prepare food, appetite, diet and nutrition;*
- *prescribed medications.*

A psychosocial assessment would include Mrs Benson's:

- *emotional and psychological well-being and mental health;*
- *safety, any fears;*
- *confidence, mood and motivation;*
- *social and interpersonal skills;*
- *ethnicity issues and cultural sensitivity;*
- *interests, leisure;*
- *reading, listening to the radio and watching TV;*
- *family and other relationships and social contacts;*
- *pets;*
- *bereavement and loss;*
- *formal and informal carers;*
- *accommodation, finance and benefits.*

→

CASE STUDY *continued*

The assessment should be supported by evidence from observation, Mrs Benson's accounts and contact with others, rather than opinion. The areas above suggest there is overlapping information to be discussed with Mrs Benson and there may be a need for a specialist assessment of certain areas before proceeding to agree a care plan with her.

Taylor and Donnelly (2006, p807) conducted a study that sought the views of health, social care and social work professionals on making decisions about the long-term care of older people. They say:

> *Decisions were often prompted by a crisis, hindering professionals seeking to make a measured assessment. Fear of burglary and assault, and the willingness and availability of family to help were major factors in decisions about living at home ... Assessment tools designed to assist decision making about the long-term care of older people need to take into account the critical aspects of individual fears and motivation, family support and the availability of publicly funded services as well as functional and medical needs.*

The SAP challenges traditional thinking about who should undertake assessments. Health practitioners may be involved in assessing adults in hospital before discharge into the community with a care package monitored by a care manager. You might be required to liaise with hospital staff to arrive at a multi-disciplinary agreement that a person is ready to be discharged from an acute hospital bed. In the past there have been tensions when doctors, sometimes at short notice, diagnosed a patient as physically fit to be discharged and care managers assessed the person as not emotionally or socially ready, or had not yet finalised a care package.

A 'delayed transfer' occurs when a patient is ready for transfer from an acute hospital bed but is still occupying it – so-called 'bed blocking'. The Community Care (Delayed Discharges etc) Act 2003 clarifies times on social services to commence assessments, places obligations on Acute Trusts to provide social services with adequate notice of the need for their services and date of discharge, and requires health and care to work jointly on this. Local authorities are liable to make a payment to the NHS for each day of a delayed discharge if arrangements have not been made by the agreed day.

Fair Access to Care Services (FACS)

FACS was guidance published by the Department of Health (2003) for local authorities to review and revise eligibility criteria for adult social care. Councils make an assessment of someone's needs with a framework such as the SAP, and use the principles in the FACS guidance to decide whether they can help people or not.

FACS provides a framework based on risks to independence that arise from people's needs relating to their:

- autonomy;

- health and safety;

- ability to manage personal and other daily routines;

- involvement in family and wider community life.

These risks can be taken into account when making an assessment of need under the NHS and Community Care Act 1990 s. 47 (1) (a). The risks relate to both immediate and long-term situations, which might deteriorate if someone is not offered help. FACS guidance prioritises the risks faced by individuals into four eligibility bands:

Critical Including threat to life, significant health problems, abuse or neglect, inability to carry out vital personal tasks and vital work or education, and a lack of vital support systems.

Substantial Including inability to carry out a majority of personal tasks and many aspects of work or education, and a lack of a majority of support systems.

Moderate Including inability to carry out several personal tasks and several aspects of work or education, and a lack of several support systems.

Low Including inability to carry out one or two personal tasks and aspects of work or education, and lack of one or two support systems.

These bands are taken into consideration when deciding whether to provide services as required by the NHS and Community Care Act 1990 s.47 (1) (b). In setting their eligibility criteria, local authorities can take into account the resources available to them. This and budget limits have resulted in most councils not offering services when need is assessed at low and moderate levels. A number offer some services when needs are assessed as substantial and there are councils whose eligibility criteria is solely at the critical level.

ACTIVITY **7.2**

An older person faces risks to her independence because she is unable to perform vital personal tasks, including washing and bathing herself.
- *Into which eligibility band would you place her needs?*
- *What do words like 'substantial', 'critical' and 'vital' in the descriptions of the bands mean to you?*

Comment

Admittedly you have very little information to go on and if you visited to make an assessment you would have a much fuller picture of the service user's ability to manage. The scenario is from FACS practice guidance implementation questions and answers (Department of Health, 2003) to show there is no hierarchy of needs. It is given as an example of *critical risks to independence* faced by the older person and compared with others that should be given equal weight (p3).

- *A younger disabled person who is facing significant obstacles in taking up the education and training that is fundamental to his independence and well being, or*
- *a single mother, with children who are often looked after by her own mother, but whose morale is severely compromised because mental health difficulties make it impossible at times for her to fulfil her parental role, which in turn exacerbates her mental health problems.*

It comments on words used that can be subjective, acknowledging that guidance can only go so far, and councils need to exercise common sense and judgement when interpreting and applying the various terms of the eligibility framework. This is something that you would face if you were carrying out assessments under this guidance.

As outlined in the last chapter, The Children Act 2004 resulted in most local authorities creating new directorates for children, families and education, separate from those dealing with adults and community care. The single mother scenario above highlights that you may be dealing with a family situation that does not fit neatly into the remit of a new council department. An implication is that you will have to communicate and work in partnership with social workers and other professionals within your local authority, as well as with those from other agencies.

Carers' assessments

We noted that a *carer's needs assessment* is one of the documents available within the SAP. The Carers (Recognition and Services) Act 1995 first recognised the role of 'informal' carers, typically a relative caring for an older, disabled or ill person, and allowed for an assessment of their ability to provide care. It was taken further with the Carers and Disabled Children Act 2000, allowing the provision of services or payments to help carers, and the Carers (Equal Opportunities) Act 2004, placing a duty on local authorities to inform carers of their right to an assessment.

Fletcher (2006, p184) points out that an assessment of carers' needs includes

> *assessing their state of health, and their wishes and ability to continue to care. To qualify for a carers' assessment, carers must be providing or intending to provide 'substantial and regular care' for another individual aged 18 or over. This assessment determines whether the carer is eligible for a 'care package' to help the person in the caring role.*

As there is no guidance definition of what 'substantial and regular care' is, Leece (2002) argues that there needs to be flexible interpretation of these terms to take into account individual carer situations and capacity to continue caring.

Seddon, et al. (2007) have been involved in an ongoing research programme into carer assessments through legislative changes. They point out there is a *considerable and enduring gap between policy and practice.* Their study (p1335) *considers practitioners' reluctance to offer separate carer assessments, identifies confusion relating to the interpretation of eligibility criteria and documents the limited contribution of health service staff.*

They highlight the need for

an evidence-based framework for good practice, that distinguishes between carer needs, service provision and carer outcomes.

CASE STUDY

Edith and Frank

Although Frank has been involved in Edith's assessment, Richard, the care manager, tells him that he is also entitled to an assessment as he cares for her a substantial amount of time and on a regular basis. Frank is very willing to care for Edith as her husband; he did not consider himself her 'carer'. However, his ability to do this is somewhat limited by his age and the fact that he has hardly undertaken practical work around the home before.

Richard asks about Frank's health and his life, including his interests. They note that there could be aids or adaptations to the home that may make things easier for both of them, particularly if Edith's mobility continues to deteriorate. The suggested care package for Edith meets a number of Frank's needs as a carer but Richard will look into the possibility of funding a carer coming in once a week for two hours to look after Edith to enable Frank to attend a local University of the Third Age (U3A) interest group.

Direct payments

When assessing a service user or carer a choice open to you is to offer cash payments directly to the individual to purchase the services that, following your assessment, you have agreed with them that they require. The facility was introduced, following campaigning from disability movements, through the Direct Payments Act 1996. Their scope has extended over time and they have become mandatory throughout the UK (Department of Health, 2008a).

Riddell, et al. (2005) analysed policy and statistics and found very low and uneven direct payments (DPs) uptake in different parts of the UK. However, there has been a rapid expansion in recent years. When assessing, you would face the dilemma that, on the one hand DPs can empower an individual by giving the person flexibility, choice and autonomy; however, the responsibility to purchase services through an agency or by becoming a carer's employer may be more than some service users want or can adequately manage.

Ellis (2007) suggests that the professional skills in assessing are important to promote access to DPs. DPs are subject to eligibility criteria and limited budgets. Ellis (2007, p409) points out that *social workers also face conflict between their legal obligation to ration access to direct payments and their ethical obligation to value self-determination and empowerment.*

The availability of DPs continues to expand. New DPs regulations (Office of Public Sector Information, 2009) state that if a person lacks capacity but has another suitable person to do so, they can be eligible to receive DPs on their behalf. Further developments, including the introduction of personal and individual budgets, are discussed below.

Safeguarding vulnerable adults

Service users, including older persons, disabled people and adults in residential care, can be vulnerable to physical, sexual, emotional, financial and institutional abuse as well as neglect. Adult protection is not drawn together into one single piece of legislation (as is protection of children in the Children Act 1989) but is contained in disparate laws relating to crimes against the person as well as policy guidance. The government published *No Secrets* (Department of Health and Home Office, 2000) guidance for local authorities to produce their own policies and procedures to respond to individual cases in multi-agency partnership. Cambridge and Parkes (2006) point out that the *No Secrets* national policy framework *has enjoyed a low profile and is permissive.* Implementation at local level has varied, including the extent of specialisation across local authorities and within teams. In 2008 the government launched a consultation on the future of adult safeguarding in England to revise the 2000 *No Secrets* guidance and to consider the need for new legislation. The results of the consultation have been published (Department of Health, 2009b) and the government is now considering a response.

In working with adults you will come across situations requiring assessment to determine whether abuse has taken place. This will demand from you the use of skills, appropriate knowledge and ethical practice. Multi-agency partnership working is absolutely key to this area of work. It may have a personal impact on you, as discussed in relation to child protection in the previous chapter. As a practitioner you will have the right to investigate even if the person concerned does not want you to do so. The scope of your duties involves a bigger picture than the individual person.

One way of safeguarding adults is through preventing people that have been involved in abuse working with them. The Department of Health regularly publishes information, materials and guidance (Department of Health, 2009e). Since October 2009 a new Independent Safeguarding Authority (ISA) has been responsible for a vetting service that has a single list of all those barred from working with vulnerable adults and another, related, list of those barred from working with children. This Barred List replaces the previous 2004 Protection of Vulnerable Adults (POVA) list.

A worker has recently become involved with Marjorie and her daughter Ellie. It is very obvious to the worker that Marjorie is finding it hard to care for her daughter, who has cerebral palsy. Initially when the worker tried to talk to her about her relationship with her daughter and being a carer she said 'everything is fine'. Ellie tells the worker she has to spend most of her time in her bedroom and her mum will not buy her the things she wants. Ellie also discloses that her mum sometimes hits her. (Pritchard, 2007, p197)

If you were the worker or a member of a local authority team receiving a referral arising from this scenario, you would have to follow your agency's policy. This will involve discussion with your manager and an initial safeguarding strategy meeting within a few days. In some cases this might be a 'virtual' meeting through telephone contact with relevant agencies, including the police. A consideration must be whether a criminal offence may have taken place. In more serious situations agency representatives will meet and may agree a visit is needed to interview those involved and to make a risk assessment. If abuse is confirmed, a case conference and protection plan would follow ideally within 10 to 14 days, although it can be longer. The plan would need to be monitored and reviewed.

Disabilities

Current government policy concerning learning disabled persons was launched with the *Valuing People* (Department of Health, 2001b) White Paper, published 30 years after the previous White Paper on learning disability. It includes proposals for children and their families, young people and adults around four key principles:

- rights as citizens;
- real chances to be independent;
- choice in daily life;
- inclusion in local communities.

A feature of pursuing the initiatives at central and local government levels, the latter through local partnership boards, is the inclusion of learning disabled people in the planning and implementation of strategies, including the current *Valuing people now* (Department of Health, 2009d).

How familiar are you with learning disabled people through work, personal knowledge, friends, acquaintances, relatives or reading?
How independent are they, do they work and participate in other social activities?
In your view, to what extent are learning disabled people capable of being full citizens and being included in the local community?
What challenges might face you when carrying out the assessment of a learning disabled person?

Comment

The value base underpinning the four *Valuing People* principles is one that should guide your assessment practice. Some of the challenges that you will come across include listening to the individual and being person-centred; seeking out, rather than being limited by, resources; assessing needs involved in transition into adult life; and the use of direct payments or personal budgets.

CASE STUDY

Sunita, a care manager in a health/social care integrated learning disability team, has been working with 21-year-old Heather who has mild learning difficulties, towards her becoming more independent. Heather completed a social skills course at a local further education college. Sunita is aware of the Valuing Employment Now initiative (Department of Health, 2009c) and is investigating the possibility of a job coach for Heather funded through a personal budget or local authority funding for supported employment.

Sunita is listening to Heather and facilitating her aspirations. Longer-term goals include working for a local employer and getting her own accommodation. Sunita has to advocate for Heather as her parents tend to be rather protective and they do not think she can manage paid employment and living on her own.

The government has not produced a specific framework or guidance for adults with physical disabilities. It subscribes to the social (often contrasted with a medical) model of disability (Barnes and Mercer, 2005). The social model conceptualises disability as disadvantage experienced by an individual through exclusion, negative attitudes and physical barriers – a disabling society, rather than their impairment or disability, disables people. A medical, or individual, model tends to see the impairment as the person's problem. Government policy, with obvious implications for assessment, is

> *to improve the life chances of disabled people by promoting their inclusion and participation in community life, empowering them to take control over their lives. Disabled people should be able to participate in the activities other people take for granted like getting a job, travelling, raising a family or going out with friends.*

(www.dh.gov.uk/en/SocialCare/Deliveringadultsocialcare/Disability/DH_079427)

Government responsibility is coordinated by the Office for Disability Issues set up in 2005. Initiatives include direct payments, personal and individual budgets; community equipment; and raising awareness of disability issues (Department of Health, 2007b).

As a response to policy aiming to enable disabled people to have greater choice and control over the support that they receive, some councils have introduced an outcome-focused, rather than a 'needs-based' or 'resource-led', approach into their social care assessment documentation.

RESEARCH SUMMARY

As part of a study on outcomes for disabled people Foster, et al. (2008) analysed assessment and care-planning documentation in two local authority teams.

Access in and around the home; personal care and comfort (e.g. maintaining personal hygiene, sitting and bed posture), transfers, independence, social/leisure/recreation, communication, domestic/daily living activities and finance accounted for 78.5% of all desired outcomes.

Equipment/aids, help with housing/accommodation, help with financial issues, professional support (including traditional social work support provided by practitioners in the course of undertaking the assessment and liaison with other professionals) and domiciliary support accounted for 70.3% of the services provided.

This analysis suggests that the majority of outcomes and services recorded tended to cluster around a fairly narrow range of conventional social care service functions involving traditional areas of social care work and of responding to need. This is a challenge for social workers, care managers and other professionals (and service users!) to be more creative and imaginative in pursuing a social model of assessment and planning.

The personalisation agenda

In 2005 the government published a social care consultation Green Paper *Independence, Well-Being and Choice: Our Vision for the Future of Social Care for Adults in England*. This led in 2006 to the publication of the Health and Social Care White Paper *Our Health, Our Care, Our Say: A New Direction for Community Services, promising a radical and sustained shift in the way in which services are delivered – ensuring that they are more personalised* ... (Department of Health, 2006, pp6–7). Plans outlined included increased use of direct payments, personal and individual budgets, greater use of the voluntary sector and families taking responsibility for care, and new local frameworks such as Primary Care Trusts, voluntary groups and local authorities being responsible for initiatives from preventative services to intensive care. Government aims are to shift responsibility for care from organised social services to individual citizens so that people will become more capable of managing their own health and welfare.

These developments challenge the role of a social worker or care manager, the traditional assessment task and the training and qualifications needed to work within adult services and community care. The Green Paper (Department of Health, 2005, p36) referred to potential professional roles including:

- *A person-centred planning facilitator to support the person to develop their own aspirations as the basis for future service plans.*
- *A care manager working alongside the person who may need services to undertake the needs assessment and act as lead professional to case manage the care package.*

- *A care navigator* with knowledge of mainstream and specialist services, working with the person using services to develop a sustained pathway of care.
- *A care broker* who might help the individual formulate the care plan, negotiate funding and help organise and monitor services.

The ideas have been brought together in *Putting people first* (Department of Health, 2007c), a short but significant paper aimed at *the transformation of adult social care*, and a *personalised adult social care system,* followed in 2008 by *Transforming Social Care* (2008c) guidance and three-year funding allocated to local authorities.

The personalisation initiatives include the expansion of direct payments (DPs). Following assessment, individuals will increasingly be allocated funding as a *personal budget* (PB) to meet their needs. Service users can take their PB as a DP or, while retaining choice about how their needs are met, opt for the council to have the responsibility to commission the services, or a combination of the two. PBs are a good option for people who do not want the full responsibility of purchasing their care through DPs.

Individual budgets (IBs) combine resources from different funding streams to which an individual is entitled (Supporting People, Disabled Facilities Grant, Independent Living Fund, Access to Work, community equipment services) to create one service user-controlled budget. IBs aim to align assessments from the different funding streams and encourage self-assessment where appropriate. Rabiee, et al. (2009, p921) state:

> IBs can be deployed in different ways: by the service user as a cash direct payment; by the care manager; by a Trust; as an indirect payment to a third party; or can be held by a service provider.

IB pilots in 13 local authorities took place between 2005 and 2007. In a modest, early evaluation study, Rabiee, et al. (2009, p924) found that individuals thought IBs provided choice and control, and one of the most positive aspects was flexibility. They *planned to spend IBs on:*

- *transport to get out and about, go to meetings and be more involved in their communities;*
- *equipment, such as tele-care equipment;*
- *short periods of respite care at times that suited users and their families;*
- *other things that mattered to them that would not have been funded under previous support arrangements.*

The above developments involving the funding of care can lead to a 'consumer choice' approach where individuals seek the services that best meet their needs and have more control in how the money is spent. The person may make their own assessment of needs. Councils have a responsibility to safeguard their resources through monitoring that money is appropriately spent, including doing so for individuals who do not have the capacity to manage their budget, due to conditions such as dementia, and may have someone else receive payments on their behalf.

Service users may need someone to help them navigate through the variety and complexity of provision and a broker to help them put a plan together and purchase services that can include transport, housing and education as well as care. Service users can become more influential and co-designers of services.

Councils are increasingly organising services to 're-enable' individuals to manage their circumstances without or with a reduced care package. Ways to support people to manage with less direct personal care include tele-care, ranging from pendant alarms to more complex home sensor arrangements that can detect gas, water on the floor or the weight of someone falling. Call, or contact, centres can be available for help and advice 24 hours a day.

REFLECTION

- *To what extent do you consider the personalisation agenda to be about human rights, including the right to 'self-determination' and 'active citizenship'?*

- *What values do you see underpinning the initiatives?*

- *Do you think there are dangers that the developments might be imposing unfair levels of responsibility and accountability onto vulnerable people?*

- *But is a reluctance to encourage service users to be more responsible for their own care not paternalistic?*

- *Are there ways in which you could guard against this when involved in the assessment of people's needs?*

Comment

There are critics such as Ferguson (2007, p387) who states that, while personalisation *appears to involve a rejection of paternalism in social work services,* it is also congruent *with key themes of New Labour thought, including of welfare reform: individualisation, responsibilisation and the transfer of risk from the state to the individual.*

The government is promoting independent living and people speaking up about their experiences. If asked, how might service users describe their lives? For some it might be very centred on routine care activities such as a PA or carer helping them, going to a day centre and travelling back on a minibus. The personalisation message might be: 'you are getting social care to live your life, not living your life to get social care'. However, some of the government concerns also include demographic and economic pressures, a drive for improvements in public services and an emphasis on measurable outcomes.

Home care re-ablement, which some councils term 'enablement' or 're-enablement' and can overlap with intermediate care, prevention and rehabilitation, involves helping people to have the confidence and relearn or regain skills they may have lost as a result of poor health, disability or impairment, going into hospital or residential care, and to learn new skills or acquire equipment for independent living. Some re-ablement services are provided jointly with health, others within adult social care but using health expertise such as therapists.

CASE STUDY

Mr Munn (75) has returned home from hospital after a hip operation. Rather than assessing him for a traditional care package, a practitioner (who may not have a social work qualification) from the council's new enablement team arranges an intensive period of support. A physiotherapist commences rehabilitation sessions three times a day, diminishing to once a day, over six weeks. Home care services are contracted out. This builds Mr Munn's confidence and he has no need for an ongoing package of care.

This is a cultural change for traditional care management. It is helping people 'to do' rather than 'doing to or for' them. Practitioners have to learn to 'let go' their management of care. Assessment for care can no longer be undertaken as a one-off activity but requires observation over a defined period of time. Councils are designing assessment tools to measure personal care and daily living skills, building confidence, household tasks, mobility, coping with poor memory, social and leisure activities. This maximises service users' independence, choice and quality of life and minimises ongoing home care and support.

RESEARCH SUMMARY

The Department of Health's Care Services Efficiency Delivery (CSED) programme commissioned a retrospective longitudinal study to evaluate pilot re-ablement schemes in four councils. In three of the four schemes;

- *53% to 68% left re-ablement requiring no immediate home care package;*
- *36% to 48% continued to require no home care package two years after re-ablement;*
- *in the fourth service, which operated on a selective basis, the results were significantly higher.*

Of those that required a home care package within the two years after re-ablement:

- *34% to 54% had maintained or reduced their home care package two years after re-ablement;*
- *in the fourth service, operating on a selective basis, the results were higher.*

Of those aged below 65 years that required a home care package within the two years after re-ablement:

- *in three of the four schemes the number that had reduced their package was higher after two years than after three months;*
- *this was even more noticeable in two of the schemes for those aged under 85 years.*

Department of Health (2007a)

You may be wondering what your future might be if you decide to work in adult services and community care. The local authority still has a duty to assess and provide services. But how the services are provided is increasingly changing.

The government is now undertaking a consultation process on revision of Fair Access to Care Services (FACS) within the Putting People First policy context (Department of Health, 2009a). The promotion of more choice and control for service users encouraged by the personalisation agenda is arguably incompatible with councils determining eligibility criteria. The consultation addresses involving people more, including involvement in their assessment and deciding how money is used; and considering the FACS levels themselves and their application, taking into account diversity and equality.

In July 2009 the government published a Green Paper (Department of Health, 2009b) proposing a national care service in which everyone who meets a new England-wide eligibility criteria will be entitled to some funding for their personal care. This would end self-funding by those with higher means and council's ability to set their own eligibility criteria level. The government would contribute to financial support from existing funding sources so the paper puts forward for consultation three approaches – partnership, insurance and comprehensive models – of how individuals would contribute to their care costs.

C H A P T E R   S U M M A R Y

This chapter explored assessment within adult services and community care starting with the legislative context and introducing you to care management and the role of care managers. Relevant national developments included the National Service Framework (NSF) for Older People, including what it says about diversity; the Single Assessment Process (SAP), for joint health/care assessments of need; and the Fair Access to Care Services (FACS) framework of risks to independence, eligibility bands and their interpretation.

We noted legislation and eligibility for carers' assessments and direct payments. We saw that adult protection policies and procedures depend on government guidance rather than legislation, as is the case for child protection. Having illustrated the above initiatives, particularly as they apply to older persons, we moved on to consider learning and physical disability.

The chapter ended with an outline of the government's personalisation agenda, new funding ideas, and the developments of services such as re-ablement, to encourage service users to have more autonomy, choice, control and independence.

FURTHER READING

Glasby, J and Littlechild, R (2009) *Direct payments and personal budgets: Putting personalisation into practice.* 2nd edition. Bristol: Policy Press.
This book reviews the origins and development of cash-for-care initiatives, suggesting they are now set to transform the whole of adult social care. It summarises current evidence and implications for policy and practice.

Hunter, S and Ritchie, P (2007) *Co-production and personalisation in social care: Changing relationships in the provision of social care.* London: Jessica Kingsley Publishers (Research highlights in social work series).
This textbook presents co-production as a model of practice in which service providers work with service users in the provision of services. Exploring theory and practice, it gives examples from housing and restorative justice as well as social care.

Means, R, Richards, S and Smith, R (2008) *Community care: Policy and practice*. 4th edition. London: Palgrave Macmillan.
This edition includes developments and reforms in community and social care up to publication date, while also outlining the historical background. It reviews health/care partnerships in practice.

WEBSITES

www.dh.gov.uk/en/SocialCare/DH_078755
The Social Care directorate of the Department of Health is a good starting point for government developments and initiatives.

www.dhcarenetworks.org.uk/
The Department of Health's DH Care Networks take the lead for the Putting People First team and personalisation agenda.

www.valuingpeople.gov.uk/
The Valuing People strategy for people with learning disabilities has its own website.

www.officefordisability.gov.uk/
The Office for Disability Issues coordinates the government's policy and strategy for disabled people.

www.in-control.org.uk
In Control, a charity and independent company, was set up in 2003 and designed self-directed support, which has been taken up by the Government. The website has a useful database of publications and technical information.

Chapter 8
Mental health

5.1.4 Social work theory.
- Models and methods of assessment, including factors underpinning the selection and testing of relevant information, the nature of professional judgement and the processes of risk assessment.

5.1.5 The nature of social work practice.
- The factors and processes that facilitate effective inter-disciplinary, inter-professional and inter-agency collaboration and partnership.

Problem-solving skills.

5.5.1 Gathering information.
- Gather information from a wide range of sources and by a variety of methods, for a range of purposes. These methods should include electronic searches using the internet, reviews of relevant written materials, face-to-face, written and telephone contact with individuals and groups.
- Take into account differences of viewpoint in gathering information and assess the reliability and relevance of the information gathered.

5.5.3 Analysis and synthesis.
- Analyse information gathered, weighing competing evidence and modifying their viewpoint in light of new information, then relate this information to a particular task, situation or problem.

5.6 Communication skills.
- Listen actively to others, engage appropriately with the life experiences of service users, understand accurately their viewpoint and overcome personal prejudices to respond appropriately to a range of complex personal and interpersonal situations.

5.7 Skills in working with others.
- Consult actively with others, including service users, who hold relevant information or expertise.

Introduction

This chapter will explore assessment in mental health social work. For adult service users it can be considered within the adult services and community care statutory framework discussed in the previous chapter. However, mental health assessment is not confined to adult social work. Children and young people may also need such assessment, typically provided within Children and Adolescents Mental Health Services (CAMHS). We will look at the legislative context, review recent developments and approaches and explore the role of the social worker in this multi-disciplinary aspect of work.

A consideration of terms may be helpful here. Since this book is about social work assessment, this chapter will not cover diagnoses of *mental disorders or psychiatric illnesses* in any depth. The term *mental health* is commonly used as, for instance, in *Community Mental Health Teams (CMHTs) and CAMHS* – multi-disciplinary teams that include social workers. Mental health social workers deal with the social and personal needs of people experiencing *mental ill health* and may intervene to help with *mental health difficulties* or *mental health problems. Mental health* – something we all experience – is a positive term and concept as opposed to the more negative connotations of illness, problems and difficulties – which we may also experience at certain points in our lives.

Having said that, as a social worker practising in this area you would be working with other professionals, and service users, who do know the diagnostic criteria and categories well. You will, therefore, need to have some understanding and a degree of proficiency about psychiatric definitions and treatments.

- *List people you know directly or indirectly (relatives, friends, people you have heard of, including in the media) who have experienced mental ill health or mental health problems, and what their condition is or was if you know it.*
- *How long is your list?*
- *What conditions does it include?*
- *What are your reactions and feelings towards the people you listed?*

Comment

Your list may be longer than you expected and might include people close to you and well-known personalities, currently living and from history, who are or have been known to experience mental health difficulties. The Office of National Statistics (ONS, 2000) states that one in six adults at any one time experience mental distress. Goldberg and Huxley (1992), probably using a wider definition, put the figure as one in four. This suggests your list should include some people close to you.

You may have included what might be considered severe and enduring psychiatric illnesses such as schizophrenia, bi-polar disorder (sometimes commonly referred to as manic depression), obsessive-compulsive disorder and dementias, as well as arguably less severe conditions including some forms of depression and anxiety that are nevertheless very distressing for the individuals concerned.

Did you have mixed feelings in your reactions to the people you listed? It is not uncommon for us to have fears or worries about people who are considered mentally ill. This may sometimes equate to fear of the unknown. As someone reading a textbook about social work assessment, one would hope that you are not among those who have negative attitudes towards mental ill health. Sadly, the history and ideology relating to mental health shows that it creates considerable suspicion and wariness (Sheldon and Macdonald, 2009, p279). As we will see below concerning the debate about community treatment orders prior to the Mental Health Act 2007, there was a view that mental health patients in the community were dangerous people who should be supervised or controlled. Some people with mental health problems may, in fact, be violent. A number of homicides and well-publicised child deaths have been committed by people with mental health problems. However, these are a minority of the large numbers of people who experience mental distress.

Working to statutory requirements

The Mental Health Act (MHA) 1983 has until recently been the main piece of legislation in this area of work. It includes definitions, powers to detain persons in hospital under sections of the Act (commonly referred to as 'sectioning'), types of discharge, rights to appeal and other matters concerning treatment. After some years of consultation and discussion, the 1983 Act has been amended, but not superseded, by the

Mental Health Act (MHA) 2007. Three amendments are of particular interest for social workers.

The MHA 1983 required an *approved social worker* (ASW), an experienced social worker that had undertaken additional training, to interview patients and recommend compulsory hospital detention jointly with two doctors. The MHA 2007 has replaced the ASW with an *approved mental health professional* (AMHP) that might include nurses, psychologists and occupational therapists, as well as social workers, thus widening the range of professionals that can be involved and emphasising a multi-disciplinary approach.

The MHA 1983 required a *responsible medical officer* (RMO) to make the decision about continuation of compulsion after a patient was detained under a limited time order of the Act. The MHA 2007 has replaced this with a *responsible clinician* (RC), allowing the RC role to be undertaken by nurses, psychologists, occupational thera-pists or social workers, as well as doctors. This decision is taken having made an assessment that the mental disorder is of a nature or degree to justify it. The new role is a considerable widening of the multi-disciplinary concept.

In the consultations and discussions leading to the MHA 2007, a *community treat-ment order* (CTO) (or *supervised community treatment*) was hotly debated as a provision relating to the controversial perceived danger of some mental health patients in the community. In the event, the CTO requires the patient to be detained under a prior section of the MHA 1983 before the order can be made. It includes a power to recall the patient and, to a limited extent, to treat the patient without their consent.

Important sections of the MHA 1983 are retained, especially as regards assessment. The MHA 1983 allows patients to be detained with certain conditions and safeguards under the following sections:

- sect 2 – for up to 28 days for assessment;
- sect 3 – for up to six months for treatment;
- sect 4 – admission for assessment in cases of emergency;
- sect 5 – in-patients may be detained for periods of either 6 or 72 hours to prevent them leaving hospital when a full assessment is necessary.

For sections 2, 3 and 4 admissions, the patient has to be examined by two doctors, one approved under the MHA 1983 and another where practicable with previous acquaintance with the patient. The person must also be interviewed by an AMHP who applies for the admission. The assessment is a team responsibility.

The MHA 2007 defines mental disorder as *any disorder or disability of the mind* widening the 1983 definitions and using a description that would seem to include learning disability and personality disorders.

Barber, et al. (2009, p1) question the need for separate mental health law, saying

... one could argue that there might be a need for law relating to mental incapacity (e.g. for people with brain injury, dementia, learning disability) but no need for a law that allows for the detention and compulsory treatment of people just because a doctor considers them to be suffering from mental illnesses (such a schizophrenia or depression). They should be treated in the same way as anyone with a physical illness such as diabetes.

An argument against this view is that it may be necessary at times to intervene against someone's will where that person is assessed as suffering from a mental disorder, either to protect others or to protect the person concerned. Interestingly, there is now legislation other than MHAs concerning the assessment of a person's mental capacity and responsibility.

Mental Capacity Act

Although included in this chapter and having the word 'mental' in its title, the Mental Capacity Act (MCA) 2005 applies to any person aged 16 and over who lacks the capacity to make decisions for whatever reason. It also allows any adult to make arrangements for a time when they may lack the capacity to make decisions in the future. The Act gives the power for decisions to be made for and on behalf of someone who lacks the capacity to do so and should be considered by anyone providing care or treatment, be they informal carers or professionals, including social workers.

A person must be assumed to have capacity unless it is established that they lack it. If all practicable steps to help a person make a decision have been taken without success, a decision may be made under the Act and must be made in the person's best interests. MCA code of practice guidance urges the use of the MCA rather than the MHA wherever possible.

CASE STUDY

Mrs Garcia (67) is severely visually impaired, though not totally blind, and was diagnosed some years ago as having bi-polar disorder. She is widowed and lives with her 39-year-old son Marc in a house she owns. Marc drinks excessively and his GP describes him as an alcoholic, although Marc does not accept this. There are concerns about the state of the house. It is dirty with urine, faeces and vomit. Mother and son often buy take-away meals, eat half the food and leave the rest in the lounge or kitchen to eat on subsequent days, which they do without reheating. After heavy drinking, Marc is often sick in paper or plastic bags, which are left about the house.

There was communication between the GP and an environmental health officer that visited the home, resulting in a referral to the CMHT. At a team meeting the referral was allocated to Inge, a social worker. Inge called to make an assessment and, using interpersonal skills, encouraged Mrs Garcia to talk about herself, her home, her health, her routines and her relationship with her son. Inge also used observation to note the condition of the property. She found that Mrs Garcia manages her bi-polar condition well

→

with medication and seemed quite rational talking about her situation, although it appeared that, possibly due to her visual impairment, she was not fully aware of the extent of dirt and health hazards in the house. She said she loves her son 'to bits', wants to care for him and does not want to ask him to leave. She admitted he could be difficult when he comes home drunk but accepts his behaviour. In discussion about this she told Inge that Marc has not been violent towards her. He tried to kiss her in the mouth once and she objected to this because she did not like his bushy beard. She interpreted his behaviour as a sign of affection.

Comment

In making this assessment, Inge used appropriate communication skills and accepted what Mrs Garcia was telling her non-judgementally to form as clear a picture as possible of the situation and to ascertain Mrs Garcia's wishes. Inge was informed and guided by legislation. She also discussed the information she gathered and her professional judgements with her team manager and professional colleagues from other disciplines. There seemed to be no need for Mrs Garcia to be detained in hospital for assessment or treatment under one of the sections of the MHA 1983 listed earlier. Section 7 of the MHA 1983 enables an application to be made to the local authority for guardianship (whether or not a person is, or has been, detained under the Act) to enable someone to receive care within the community when it cannot be provided without the use of compulsion. However, this did not seem appropriate at this stage.

Under the MCA 2005 Inge had to assess whether Mrs Garcia lacked the capacity to decide to live under her current conditions or ask her son to leave. A principle of this Act is that a person is not to be treated as unable to make a decision merely because they make an unwise decision. Mrs Garcia seemed to be consenting to living as she was and to understand what she was doing. Through questioning Mrs Garcia about how she cared for herself and sensitively asking about Marc's behaviour toward her, Inge undertook a mental health risk assessment, including risk of self-neglect and sexual risks. She considered using safeguarding of vulnerable adults procedures to meet Mrs Garcia's needs. Inge assessed that Mrs Garcia's mental ill health was not a primary concern and will consider making a referral to the local authority older persons care management team. While in contact with Mrs Garcia monitoring and evaluating the situation, she will also ask to see Marc and may refer him to a substance misuse team if he consents. She will take these considerations for discussion to her multi-disciplinary team meeting.

National developments in mental health

The National Service Framework (NSF) for Mental Health was published in 1999. It set out a ten-year programme to promote mental health and encourage access to services at primary care level. It included guidance for the provision of services for those with severe mental illnesses, and standards relating to caring for carers and preventing suicide.

Mental health is an area where health and social services practitioners have worked in partnership for some time. CMHTs, some originally known as Primary Care Liaison Teams, have evolved over the past 25 years or so as a result of a trend towards care in non-hospital settings. A mental health implementation guide in 2001 saw them as the mainstay of the system, and a mental health policy implementation guide about CMHTs (Department of Health, 2002b, p8) suggested *most assessments of those with severe mental illness should involve trained medical staff* and *those with common mental health problems may more appropriately be assessed by other team members.* It pointed out that

> *social work assessment takes place within the framework of the Care Programme Approach, which is Care Management for those of working age in contact with specialist mental health and social services.*

> *Each service user is assigned a care co-ordinator with overall CPA responsibility for ensuring appropriate assessment, care and review by themselves and others in the team.*

The Care Programme Approach (CPA), initially introduced in 1991, was reviewed in 2006 and is now being refocused (Department of Health, 2008b). As a framework that supports and coordinates effective mental health care, the CPA has been applied at two levels:

- standard support;
- enhanced support.

The proposal now is that the CPA should not apply to less complex cases but that it should be used in secondary mental health care as an approach to assessing, planning, reviewing and coordinating treatment, care and support. Assessing risks and appointing a care coordinator remain important elements. These developments fit in with those that apply to adult service users discussed in the previous chapter. Thus *personalised* mental health care is advocated with assessment of care needs against FACS eligibility criteria and with the availability of direct payments and individual budgets. Although they should be offered, management of DPs and IBs, as we noted in the previous chapter, depends on a mental health service user being willing and able to take financial control of their care.

Practice settings

As a social worker in a CMHT, you might be seconded to or employed by a Mental Health NHS Trust. Different CMHTs will have separate functions or be divided into specialisms. Most Trusts have intake or access teams where nursing or medical practitioners will mainly undertake the assessment and short-term treatment. There may be early and crisis intervention teams, which can be hospital-based, and enhanced and assertive outreach teams. CMHTs will usually include consultant psychiatrists, community psychiatric nurses (CPNs), occupational therapists (OTs), social workers, care managers and other professionals such as clinical psychologists.

There are different pathways to assessment. A CMHT dealing with severe and enduring mental ill health may receive a referral from an intake team and make a decision within the CPA framework whether a CPN, OT or social worker should undertake an assessment of need and a mental health risk assessment. Mental health needs may relate to children, older persons and people with a learning disability. As mentioned earlier, the multi-disciplinary approach has been reinforced by the MHA 2007 to the extent that AMHPs are now involved in MHA assessments.

RESEARCH SUMMARY

Hatfield (2008) undertook a study of individuals assessed by ASWs under the MHA with a view to hospital detention over nine years in six local authorities, developing a profile of the individuals and reviewing the role of the ASW.

The number of men assessed and detained overall exceeded the numbers of women. However, the gender dimension interacted with age so that more men than women were assessed up to age 40. The figures showed that in the group aged 40 and above, more women than men were assessed. The most common marital status recorded was 'single'. Poor material resources, isolation and drug and alcohol misuse were key features that may be associated with mental health need. There was a close association evident between psychiatric severity and social disadvantage. Only two of the six local authorities had total minority populations exceeding 6% in the 2001 census. In one of these there was a marked over-representation of MHA assessments involving people described as African-Caribbean, but not of other minority groups.

The study leads Hatfield (2008) to suggest that mental health social workers are uniquely equipped to identify issues in the social context that may contribute to mental health crisis. She argues that the ASW role brought a dimension to the decision to detain someone in hospital that is based upon social perspectives and a social assessment, balancing the medical assessment. ASWs brought assessment skills that took account of relationship dynamics, factors in the social context such as housing, employment and poverty, and the impact on individuals of life events. They also brought cultural competence with an awareness of the impact of issues such as race, language and culture in the context of mental ill health.

Some social workers regret the demise of the ASW role in favour of the AMHP instituted by the MHA 2007. There is concern that the medical tradition and hierarchical culture is such that nurses, for instance, defer to consultants and may not be as independent an 'applicant' as ASWs largely were.

Factors relating to race and culture

Black and minority ethnic (BME) service users, and particularly men of African-Caribbean origin, are over-represented in the figures of those diagnosed with mental illness, compulsory admittance to hospital and in admissions involving police officers. Active discrimination seems to be evident, although there may be a complexity of interacting factors. Sheldon and Macdonald (2009, p288) suggest that

> *minority ethnic clients are far less likely to have had access to culturally sympathetic preventive services. Thus, screening, early intervention, suitable medication and relapse-prevention follow-up are much less likely to be present in such cases.*

Fernando (2002) clarifies the use of the term *race* characterised by physical appearance, determined by genetic ancestry and perceived as permanent. *Culture* is characterised by behaviour and attitudes, determined by upbringing and choice, and perceived as changeable. *Ethnicity* is characterised by a sense of belonging and group identity, determined by social pressures and psychological need and perceived as partially changeable.

All mental health practitioners, and social workers in particular, must be aware of the stress effects of racism experienced by BME service users. Behaviour and attitudes that are culturally diverse can be misrepresented and misunderstood compounding the stigma and negative responses that many people experiencing mental ill health encounter. A sense of isolation, alienation and not belonging may be prevalent in some ethnic groups, thus exacerbating mental health problems for some individuals.

Mental health social work

As a mental health social worker you are likely to be making assessments based on a psycho-social approach, addressing needs such as the loneliness of someone without a family, social isolation and exclusion, factors relating to race, culture and ethnicity, vocational advice, accommodation and housing problems and financial help through benefits. In addition, you would assess how social issues impact on the mental health and psychological well-being of the person. Following the assessment you would be deciding whether a service, including the involvement of support workers, can and will be offered. This is not unlike the role of a care manager. However, mental health service users do not pay for their care packages.

The above suggests the typical role of a social worker. At a CMHT allocation meeting a CPN, for instance, might be the practitioner more likely allocated to assess a service user in a psychotic state not taking their medication. In a team approach the skills and professional interests of each worker, whatever their discipline, can be taken into account. You might develop an interest and specialism in areas such as postnatal depression, cognitive behavioural therapy (CBT) or motivational interviewing.

As a mental health social worker you are playing a part in team assessment and might contribute a social history or chronology. A multi-disciplinary approach can enable different levels of assessment to be tailored to individual needs. Assessment is based on the understanding that different people function in different ways and is part of starting to work with the person, realising that intervention will not last for ever.

Most mental health practitioners work to a 'recovery model' advocated by the National Mental Health Development Unit, formally National Institute for Mental Health in England (NIMHE, 2005). It is strengths, rather than deficits, based and focuses on the person, not just their symptoms. In this way of working you would involve the person in their assessment as an expert on themselves. The process or conceptual framework of recovery is aimed at enabling a person to stay in control of their life despite experiencing a mental health problem and to understand the lived experience of recovery (Repper and Perkins, 2003). At one level this approach supports social work values, allowing a service user autonomy and promoting their empowerment. However, there is a danger that government initiatives can be driven by economic considerations and by targets such as reducing the number of people claiming incapacity benefit and increasing the numbers that obtain employment. A recovery model assumes a person accepts intervention, agrees there are risks and wants to cooperate towards achieving a personally acceptable quality of life.

CASE STUDY

Mr Symmes (66) was diagnosed with schizophrenia a number of years ago. As a quantity surveyor he worked in many parts of the world and enjoyed a comfortable lifestyle. He now lives in a housing association property and seems to be well off financially, although he does not disclose whether he has a pension, savings or borrows money. His family moved to Australia and he is on his own. He is an intelligent man who has been competitive in business and leisure interests such as long-distance cycling.

The housing association reports problems with neighbours. Mr Symmes is said to be rude to others about neighbour disputes. He speaks in an intimidating way and has resorted to litigation as a way of tackling disagreements. Female neighbours have reported experiencing sexual harassment from him consisting of stalking them and inappropriate language amounting to psychological abuse. They describe him as considering himself a 'ladies man'.

In spite of the above background that suggests self-assurance, Mike, a mental health social worker, established a relationship with Mr Symmes, engaged him in talking about himself and noted low self-esteem and despair. Mike assessed Mr Symmes as a high suicide risk and has been the applicant in MHA assessments that have resulted in section 3 detentions in hospital for treatment. Mr Symmes does not automatically acknowledge a mental health problem and does not accept his behaviour is offensive to others, but he becomes much more self-aware after a period of hospital medication and is initially reasonable with his neighbours when he returns home. He has a pattern of his behaviour deteriorating when he is out of hospital. Following a number of compulsory admissions under previous legislation, he is now on a MHA 2007 community treatment order while still under sect. 3 of the MHA 1983.

Mike is involved in ongoing review and continuous assessment. Mr Symmes' situation highlights the question of who defines the goals of recovery. To neighbours, Mr Symmes' 'recovery' following treatment is rather modest and temporary. Mr Symmes himself seems to enjoy a combative relationship with neighbours and the pursuit of women. In working with him Mike has to find common ground, otherwise it is difficult for him to accept Mr Symmes' self-perceptions as those of an expert on himself. He has a good relationship with Mike and is grateful for practical help such as arranging for Mr Symmes' cat and budgies to be looked after when he is in hospital.

Assessment tools

Mental Health NHS Trusts have their own documentation for needs and risk assessments with given categories for the assessor to comment on, with the danger that they can become a 'tick-box' approach. In 1993 the Department of Health commissioned the Royal College of Psychiatrists to develop scales to measure the health and social functioning of people with mental ill health. Development and testing resulted in an instrument with 12 items measuring behaviour, impairment and social functioning (Wing, et al., 1996). These Health of the Nation Outcome Scales (HoNOS) are increasingly being adopted by mental health services for assessment.

It could be argued that a narrow data-collection classification and diagnostic approach is incompatible with a recovery model aimed at obtaining a holistic picture of the individual being assessed. A skill for assessors is to work with the required tools but use them flexibly to empathetically understand the person before them.

CASE STUDY

David, a newly qualified social worker in a CMHT, asked his more experienced colleague Cristina to sit in on an assessment he was undertaking of 25-year-old Hannah, a single parent of two young children referred by her GP following an attempted suicide. Asking a female colleague to be present was part of the team's policy on gender awareness.

While David was following the headings in the needs assessment form, asking Hannah about her family, housing and environment, financial situation, social skills and self-care, she started to cry, wiping her eyes and nose with the back of her hand. Conscious of the gender difference, David felt at a loss as to how to respond and continued asking questions, working down the list of headings in the form.

Cristina sensitively intervened, asked Hannah whether she was OK to continue and offered her a tissue. She asked her open questions about how she was feeling about herself and how she managed her family and home responsibilities. In her general answers Hannah gave information relevant to some of the specific questions in the needs assessment form.

Assessment of carers

As mentioned in the previous chapter concerning adult services and community care, legislation promotes the assessment of carers' needs and allows the provision of services or payments to meet them. The carer of a service user experiencing mental ill health, such as a spouse, may feel excluded from decisions concerning their loved one's treatment. In some CMHTs there may be a specialist care manager who undertakes carers' assessments. A service that may be needed and welcomed could be a period of respite. Manktelow (2008, p268) suggests that

> *The primary focus of work for the mental health social worker is the family who are often the main carers of people with enduring mental illness.*

> *Carers' experience is often one of lonely isolation with infrequent social work contact. In these circumstances, carers' groups are an essential form of support offering a safe opportunity to share worries and fears, and the potential to form a consumer campaign to demand improved services.*

NHS finance differs from that of local authorities but many trusts have a dedicated carers' budget and support carers' associations.

Treatment of persons convicted of crimes

Section 37 of the MHA 1983 is a treatment order similar to section 3, which applies to persons convicted of crimes punishable by imprisonment. A court can impose the treatment order as an alternative to prison. For those offenders with a history of dangerous behaviour or who have committed a particularly serious offence, the court can also use section 41, in conjunction with section 37, making the Ministry of Justice, rather than medical practitioners, responsible for the decision as to when the person can leave hospital.

As a mental health social worker you may supervise a person conditionally discharged under sections 37/41, monitor their progress and make a risk assessment if their behaviour gives cause for concern. It would be your responsibility to raise the alarm, involve a consultant and refer someone to the Ministry of Justice for recall to hospital.

CASE STUDY

Maryse, a senior social work practitioner in a CMHT, has been supervising a sex offender discharged from hospital under sections 37/41 of the MHA 1983. Maryse became aware that he started drinking excessively after several months in the community. She exercised her professional judgement about the risk he was posing. His ex-partner notified her that he had attacked her and sexually assaulted her in front of her young child.

At this point Maryse raised the alarm, visited him jointly with a medical consultant and referred him to the Ministry of Justice for recall to hospital.

REFLECTION POINT

Reflect on your answers to the questions in Activity 8.1 at the start of this chapter.
Have your views changed to any extent?
If you were uncertain about this service user group due to fear of the unknown, has the
knowledge gained through reading this chapter lessened your fear?
What have been some of the significant themes in this chapter for you?
Would you consider working with this service user group?

Comment

As with other service user groups, assessment can be at different levels and for different purposes. It is not a once-and-for-all activity but an ongoing and continuous one. A multi-disciplinary approach is a feature in mental health, particularly with health and social work professionals working in partnership. This is a service user group that has experienced stigma and negative attitudes for many years. It can include a few people that have been violent, dangerous and offenders. You may come across people that do not easily accept help. There are no easy solutions. However, the service user group represents a cross-section of the population and will include colleagues, relatives, friends and perhaps you and me.

C H A P T E R   S U M M A R Y

This chapter introduced you to assessment in mental health with its own legislative context and practice settings. The Mental Capacity Act 2005 is an example of legislation that applies to all adult service users. Relevant national developments included the 1991 Care Programme Approach (CPA), now being refocused, and the 1999 National Service Framework (NSF) for Mental Health.

We explored the multi-disciplinary nature of work in CMHTs and CAMHS, and the distinctive role that social workers can play in assessment and other areas of work. We saw how an awareness of the concepts of *race*, *culture* and *ethnicity* can help you understand and work with a service user group that already faces negative attitudes and discrimination. The chapter gave examples of generic skills and knowledge appropriate to work in mental health but highlighted approaches, such as the *recovery model*, specific to this area of work.

The chapter ended with a reminder that the assessment of carers, as with other service user groups, is also relevant to mental health and that work with offenders is an aspect of statutory work in mental health.

FURTHER READING

Barber, P, Brown, R and Martin, D (2009) *Mental health law in England and Wales: A guide for mental health professionals.* Exeter: Learning Matters.
An excellent review of legislation and regulations, applied to practice. It includes the MHA 2007 amendments, the MCA 2005 and its interface with the MHA.

Burns, T (2004) *Community mental health teams: A guide to current practices.* Oxford: OUP.
Although not specifically from a social work viewpoint, this book is a useful introduction to a multi-disciplinary approach and types of CMHTs.

Fernando, S (2001) *Mental health, race and culture*. 2nd edition. London: Palgrave Macmillan.
This is a thorough exploration of the implications of race, culture and ethnicity for mental health
and psychiatry. It outlines Asian and African approaches and technologies that might lead to a
redefinition of mental illness and promote mental health for all.

Sheldon, B and Macdonald, G (2009) Social work and mental health. Chapter 13, in *A textbook of
social work*. London: Routledge.
This chapter is a brief but helpful and research-based introduction to mental health history,
ideology and government policies; factors, including socio-cultural ones, in mental disorders; and
outlines of common mental health conditions and disorders.

WEBSITES

www.nmhdu.org.uk/
Initiatives from the Department of Health and the NHS to implement mental health policy are
coordinated by the National Mental Health Development Unit launched in April 2009.

www.mind.org.uk/
The National Association for Mental Health charity, MIND, provides relevant information, news and
summaries of government developments.

www.mentalhealth.org.uk/
As a long-standing UK charity, the Mental Health Foundation is a useful source of information and
research.

www.sumanfernando.com/
The personal website of Suman Fernando provides information on issues of 'race' and 'culture' in
relation to mental health.

Conclusion

This book has explored an assortment of ingredients that can be part of the mixture that is assessment in social work practice. As you have read the preceding chapters, or even if you have dipped into sections of them, you will probably agree by now that the practice of social work assessment is complex, involving a diversity of skills, knowledge and values. We have seen that assessment is not one easily outlined activity but a continuous and often multi-faceted process that can be more or less formal, more or less objective, brief and initial or core and comprehensive. We also noted that assessment is not a discreet, time-limited event, but an integral part of the cyclical, ongoing, fluid and dynamic 'Assessment, Planning, Intervention and Review' social work process.

Chapter 1 highlighted that assessment can be defined in a variety of ways. A technical view of it focuses on its process, frameworks, questions to ask and procedures to follow. It is also possible to characterise assessment as contingent, or dependent, on the type of service being offered, the goals you are aiming to achieve and its theoretical underpinning. Another focus is the contestation or conflict between the needs of the person being assessed, the eligibility criteria used by and resources available to your agency, and your idealism in wanting to meet need. A fourth viewpoint is a critical social constructionism one, reminding us that the act of assessment involves the social construction of meanings and interpretations of problems and need.

During and as a result of assessments you will be required to make difficult decisions. These are not highly predictive, like undertaking a blood test to diagnose a disease. Objective, clear and explicit analytic reasoning will be involved in helping you reach conclusions. However, assessment may also involve an intuitive reasoning element associated with creativity and imagery that can be present in the empathetic understanding of complexity in human interactions. We noted that social work assessment can be thought of as both an art and a science.

Chapters 2, 3 and 4 addressed skills needed for assessment, alternative theoretical approaches and values underpinning assessment. The skills we reviewed were basic interpersonal ones, fundamental for social work practice, and we applied them particularly to assessment. Some skills, such as those involved in investigative assessment, are more specific to the subject of this textbook.

In outlining areas of knowledge and theoretical models that can inform assessment, we reviewed approaches such as psychodynamic, humanistic and ecological perspectives that help us generally understand human motivation and need within a systemic framework. We also reviewed behavioural approaches and task-centred and solution-focused modes of practice that more specifically underpin intervention methods.

Chapter 4 highlighted the professional social work value base underpinning assessment and the power balance between assessor and the person being assessed. It emphasised the importance for social work practice of assessments being undertaken in a way that respects the humanity of those being assessed.

Chapter 5 provided a generic exploration of assessment of risk in social work. In the context of how risk is regarded in society generally and some of the views for and against the concept of a 'risk society', we reviewed the contributions of actuarial and clinical approaches to assessing risk in social work. The chapter stressed that assessment and prediction of risk is by no means a straightforward matter. In an analysis of 45 child abuse inquiry reports in Britain between 1973 and 1994, Munro (1999, p754) reminds us that:

> *Risk assessment instruments, for example, can be invaluable aids but they cannot provide a satisfactory replacement for professional judgement. The statistical problems of predicting rare events combined with the limited knowledge of predictive factors for abuse mean that any instrument, used in an actuarial manner, will produce an unacceptably high level of inaccuracy. Browne estimated that, on existing knowledge of risk factors, if we screen 10,000 children in the general population, we would miss seven high risk cases, correctly identify 33 and falsely identify another 1,195 families as high risk.* (Browne and Saqi, 1988)

An objective assessment should lead to professional judgements and conclusions. However, the difficult decisions that social workers have to make are by no means always clear-cut. In a 2003–5 biennial analysis of serious case reviews, which must be held when a child has suffered serious injury or has died, Brandon, et al. (2008, p106) state:

> *The analysis of the reviews has shown that the numbers of factors that interact and increase and decrease the risk of harm to children are extremely complex. Even if the 'whole picture' of family circumstances had been known, it would not have been possible to accurately factor in and compute a clear outcome for most of the children at the centre of the reviews ... The complexity of many of the reviews studied means that most cases of serious harm may be essentially unpredictable. Thus living with uncertainty and risk is at the core of work with children and families – a further reason that good support is needed.*

Although the above studies relate to children and families and not all assessments address life-threatening situations, the comments highlight the complexity of factors and unpredictability of situations that face all social workers and care managers.

In Chapters 6, 7 and 8 we applied the generic areas outlined in previous chapters to the task of assessing various service user groups in children's services, adults and community care and mental health. The aim of these chapters was to give you guidance to undertake assessments in the context of changing social work practice. They explored implications of contemporary legislation and government policies and initiatives leading towards person-centred practice and service users taking increasing responsibility for their own assessments. This included the *Every Child Matters* agenda for children and families and the *Putting People First* and personalisation agenda for adults. A recurring additional theme was that social work assessment takes place, as Unit 17 of the NOS for Social Work states, in multi-disciplinary and multi-organisational teams, networks and systems. A general finding from Munro (1999, p745) was that *professionals based assessments of risk on a narrow range of evidence. It was biased towards the information readily available to them, overlooking significant data known to other professionals.*

The practice-based examples and case studies in this book are there to help you apply the ideas to practice situations and to encourage you to reflect on the implications of the complexity of assessment. However, the book has inevitably been no more than an introduction to assessment. It did not set out to outline specific frameworks, tools and assessment procedures in detail. Social work is in a time of change and review. You may wonder whether there is ever a time when this is not so! In recent years we have had the *Every Child Matters* agenda, *Putting People First* and personalisation agenda for adult services, the GSCC-led *Social Work at its Best: Roles and Task of Social Workers* report, the CWDC *Newly Qualified Outcome Statements and Remodelling Social Work Delivery* 2008–11 project, reports from the National Social Work Task Force, and the report of the House of Commons Children, Schools and Families Committee on the *Training of Children and Families Social Workers*.

It is relevant to consider traditional skills, knowledge and values associated with assessment in the context of changing practice. It is also important that you work beyond the introductory ideas in this book by pursuing the suggestions for further reading, exploring literature and other resources concerning assessment of specific service user groups of relevance to you, and updating yourself about new legislation, government initiatives and developments through the suggested websites and becoming aware of consultation and policy papers. This is part of your continuous professional development (CPD), which can involve you in individually researching and reading about areas of practice new to you, as well as more formal and traditional CPD activities such as attending in-service training events, courses and conferences.

As you progress through your social work degree programme and become a qualified practitioner you will experience practice placements and when you start work you will be allocated cases that require assessment. The information and ideas in this book will help you, but you will learn further from experience and interaction with colleagues and other professionals, you will develop your skills and knowledge and this should lead you to further in-depth reading of more specific textbooks, research findings and evidence-based theories. You will add to theories that help understand problems evidence from research as to what approach is likely to be more effective.

Although the book has not addressed specialised areas such as disabilities, substance misuse, asylum seekers and some medical conditions, and has not tackled the assessment of prospective foster carers and adoptive parents, do remember that there are transferable skills, theoretical approaches and values that can be applied to any facet of social work practice.

You can treat this book as a springboard to exploration of both the depth and breadth of social work assessment. Key Role 6 of the NOS for Social Work requires you to demonstrate your professional competence in social work practice. This includes researching, analysing, evaluating and using current knowledge of best social work practice (Unit 18), working within agreed standards of social work practice and ensuring your own professional development (Unit 19), managing complex ethical issues, dilemmas and conflicts that might affect your practice (Unit 20), and contributing to the promotion of best social work practice (Unit 21). All these expectations and requirements can be applied to social work assessment.

References

Ainsworth, M D S, Blehar, M C, Waters, E and Wall, S (eds) (1978) *Patterns of attachment: A psychological study of the strange situation.* Hillside, NJ: Erlbaum.

Bagarozzi, DA and Wodarski, JS (1977) A social exchange typology of conjugal relationships and conflict development. *Journal of Marriage and Family Counselling*, 3 (4), 53–8.

Banks, S (2006) *Ethics and values in social work.* 3rd edition. London: Palgrave Macmillan.

Banks, S (2008) Critical commentary: Social work ethics. *British Journal of Social Work*, 38 (6), 1238–49.

Banks, S and Williams, R (2005) Accounting for ethical difficulties in social welfare work: Issues, problems and dilemmas. *British Journal of Social Work*, 35 (7), 1005–22.

Barber, P, Brown, R and Martin, D (2009) *Mental health law in England and Wales: A guide for mental health professionals.* Exeter: Learning Matters.

Barnes, C and Mercer, G (eds) (2005) *Disability policy and practice: Applying the social model of disability.* Leeds: The Disability Press.

Barnes, J (2002) *Reform of social work education and training – Focus on the future: Key messages from focus groups about the future of social work training.* London: Department of Health. www.dh.gov.uk/en/Publicationsandstatistics/

Beck, A T (1976) *Cognitive therapy and the emotional disorders.* New York: International Universities Press.

Beck, U (1992) *The risk society: Towards a new modernity.* London: Sage.

Beckett, C and Maynard, A (2005) *Values and ethics in social work: An introduction.* London: Sage Publications.

Bernard, C (2002) Giving voice to experiences: Parental maltreatment of black children in the context of societal racism. *Journal of Child and Family Social Work*, 7 (4), 239–53.

Bernard, C and Gupta, A (2008) Black African children and the child protection system. *British Journal of Social Work,* 38 (3), 476–92.

Biestek, F P (1957) *The casework relationship.* Chicago: Loyola University Press.

Brandon, M, Belderson, P, Warren, C, Howe, D, Gardner, R, Dodsworth, J, and Black, J (2008) *Analysing child death and serious injury through abuse and neglect: What can we learn? A biennial analysis of serious case reviews 2003–2005,* Department for Children Schools and Families, Research Report RR023, Nottingham: DCSF.

Brearley, C P (1982) Risk *and social work.* London: Routledge.

Bronfenbrenner, U (1979) *The ecology of human development: Experiments by nature and design,* Cambridge, MA: Harvard University Press.

Browne, K, and Saqi, S (1988) *Early prediction and prevention of child abuse.* Chichester: Wiley.

Cambridge, P and Parks, T (2006) The tension between mainstream competence and specialization in adult protection: An evaluation of the role of the adult protection co-ordinator. *British Journal of Social Work,* 36 (2), 299–321.

Charlton, J I (1998) *Nothing about us without us: Disability oppression and empowerment.* Berkeley and Los Angeles: University of California Press.

Children's Workforce Development Council (2008) *Common assessment framework.* Leeds: CWDC. www.dcsf.gov.uk/everychildmatters/

Children's Workforce Development Council (2009) *The common assessment framework for children and young people: A guide for practitioners.* Leeds: CWDC. www.dcsf.gov.uk/everychildmatters/

Coulshed, V (1991) *Social work practice: An introduction.* 2nd edition. Basingstoke: Macmillan/ BASW.

Coulshed, V and Orme, J (2006) *Social work practice.* 4th edition. Basingstoke: Palgrave Macmillan/ BASW.

Crisp, B R, Anderson, M R, Orme, J and Lister, P G (2005) *Knowledge review 09: Learning and teaching in social work education: textbooks and frameworks on Assessment.* London: Social Care Institute for Excellence. www.scie.org.uk/publications/

Crisp, B R, Anderson, M R, Orme, J and Lister, P G (2007) Assessment frameworks: A critical reflection. *British Journal of Social Work,* 37 (6), 1059–77.

Dalrymple, J and Burke, B (1995) *Anti-oppressive practice.* Buckingham: Open University Press.

de Shazer, S (1985) *Keys to solution in brief therapy.* New York: Norton.

Department for Education and Skills (2001) *The Connexions framework for assessment, planning, implementation and review: Guidance for personal advisers.* London: DfES Publications. Crown copyright.

Department of Education and Skills (2003) *Every child matters.* Cm 5860. Norwich: HMSO. Crown copyright.

Department for Education and Skills (2006) *Working together to safeguard children.* Norwich: The Stationary Office. Crown copyright. www.dcsf.gov.uk/everychildmatters/

Department for Education and Skills (2007) *Every parent matters.* Nottingham: DfES. Publications Crown copyright. www.teachernet.gov.uk/

Department of Health (1999a) *MISC (99)50: The government's objectives for children's social services.* London: Department of Health Circular.

Department of Health (1999b) *National service framework for mental health.* London: Department of Health. Crown copyright. www.dh.gov.uk/en/Publicationsandstatistics/

Department of Health (2000) *HSC 2000/033: Quality protects programme: transforming children's services, 2001–2002.* London: Department of Health Local Authority Circular. www.dh.gov.uk/

Department of Health (2001a) *National service framework for older people.* London: Department of Health. Crown copyright. www.dh.gov.uk/en/Publicationsandstatistics/

Department of Health (2001b) *Valuing people: A new strategy for learning disability for the 21st century. Cm5086.* London: Department of Health. Crown copyright. www.dh.gov.uk/en/Publications andstatistics/Publications/

Department of Health (2002a) *An introduction to the single assessment process (SAP) for older people.* London: Department of Health.www.dh.gov.uk/en/SocialCare/

Department of Health (2002b) *Mental health policy implementation guide: Community mental health teams.* London: DH Publications. Crown copyright. www.dh.gov.uk/en/Publicationsandstat istics/

Department of Health (2003) *Fair access to care services – guidance on eligibility criteria for adult social care. Practical guidance: Implementation questions and answers.* London: Department of Health. Crown copyright. www.dh.gov.uk/en/Publicationsandstatistics/

Department of Health (2004) *National Service Framework for children, young people and maternity services.* London: DH Publications. Crown copyright.www.dh.gov.uk/en/Publicationsandstatistics/ Publications/

Department of Health. *Independence, well-being and choice: Our vision for the future of social care for adults in England.* London: Department of Health. Crown copyright. www.dh.gov.uk/en/Publica tionsandstatistics/

Deaprtment of Health (2006) *Our health, our care, our say: A new direction for community services.* London: Department of Health. Crown copyright. www.dh.gov.uk/en/Publicationsandstatistics/

Department of Health (2007a) *Homecare re-ablement: Retrospective longitudinal study.* London: Department of Health. www.dhcarenetworks.org.uk/

Department of Health (2007b) *Initiatives related to disabled people.* London: Department of Health. www.dh.gov.uk/en/SocialCare/

Department of Health (2007c) *Putting people first: A shared vision and commitment to the trans-formation of adult social care.* London: Department of Health. www.dh.gov.uk/en/Publications andstatistics/

Department of Health (2008a) *An introduction to direct payments.* London: Department of Health. www.dh.gov.uk/en/SocialCare/

Department of Health (2008b) *Refocusing the care programme approach: Policy and positive prac-tice guidance.* London: DH Publications. Crown copyright. www.dh.gov.uk/en/Publications andstatistics/

Department of Health (2008c) *Transforming social care.* London: Department of Health. Crown copyright. www.dh.gov.uk/en/Publicationsandstatistics/

Department of Health (2009a) *Consultation on the revision of the Fair Access to Care Services guidance to support councils to determine eligibility for social care services.* London: Department of Health. Crown copyright. www.dh.gov.uk/en/Consultations/

Departmant of Health (2009b) *Shaping the future of care together. Cm7673.* London: Department of Health. Crown copyright. www.dh.gov.uk/en/Publicationsandstatistics/

Department of Health (2009c) *Valuing employment now: Real jobs for people with learning dis-abilities.* London: Department of Health. Crown copyright. www.dh.gov.uk/en/Publications andstatistics/

Department of Health (2009d) *Valuing people now: A new three year strategy for people with learning disabilities.* London: Department of Health. www.dh.gov.uk/en/SocialCare/

Department of Health (2009e) *Vulnerable adults*. London: Department of Health. www.dh.gov.uk/en/SocialCare/

Department of Health (n.d.) *Disability*. London: Department of Health. www.dh.gov.uk/en/Social Care/

Department of Health and Home Office (2000) *No Secrets: Guidance on developing and implementing multi-agency policies and procedures to protect vulnerable adults from abuse*. London: Department of Health. Crown copyright. www.dh.gov.uk/en/Publicationsandstatistics/

Department of Health, Department for Education and Employment, and Home Office (2000) *Framework for the assessment of children in need and their families*. London: The Stationery Office. Crown copyright. www.dh.gov.uk/en/Publicationsandstatistics/

Department of Health, Social Services Inspectorate (1991) *Care management and assessment: Practitioners' guide*. London: DH Publications. Crown copyright.

Dutt, R and Phillips, M (2000) Assessing black children in need and their families. In Department Health et al. (eds) *Assessing children in need and their families: Practice guidance*. London: The Stationery Office.

Dwivedi, K N (2004) Introduction. In K N Dwivedi (ed) *Meeting the needs of ethnic minority children*. London: Jessica Kingsley.

Eborall, C (2003) *The state of the social care workforce in England* (Volume 1 of the first annual report of the Topss England workforce intelligence unit). Leeds: Training Organisation for the Personal Social Services England.

Egan, G (2007) *The skilled helper: A problem-management and opportunity development approach to helping*. 8th edition. London: Thomson Learning.

Ellis, A (1979) The basic clinical theory of rational-emotive therapy (RET). In Dryden, W and Golden, W (eds) *Cognitive-behavioural approaches in psychotherapy*. London: Harper & Row.

Ellis, K (2007) Direct payments and social work practice: The significance of 'street-level bureaucracy' in determining eligibility. *British Journal of Social Work*, 37 (3), 405–22.

Empson, JM and Nabuzoka, D with Hamilton, D (2004) *A typical child development in context*. Basingstoke: Palgrave MacMillan.

Erooga, M and Print, B (2001) Assessing parental capacity when intrafamilial sexual abuse by an adult is a concern, in Horwath, J (ed) *The child's world: Assessing children in need*. London: Jessica Kingsley Publishers.

FACE (2009) www.face.eu.com/

Farnfield, S (2008) A theoretical model for the comprehensive assessment of parenting. *British Journal of Social Work*. 38 (6), 1076–99.

Ferguson, I (2007) Increasing user choice or privatizing risk? The antinomies of personalization. *British Journal of Social Work,* 37 (3), 387–403.

Fletcher, M (2006) Carers and direct payments. In Leece, J and Bornat, J (eds.) *Developments in direct payments*. Bristol: Policy Press.

Fernando, S (2002) *Mental health, race and culture*. Basingstoke: Palgrave.

Fook, J (2002) *Social work: Critical theory and practice*. London: Sage Publications.

Foster, M, Harris, J, Jackson, K and Glendinning, C (2008) Practitioners' documentation of assessment and care planning in social care: The opportunities for organizational learning. *British Journal of Social Work*, 38 (3), 546–60.

Furedi, F (2008) *Paranoid parenting: Why ignoring the experts may be best for your child.* 2nd edition. London: Continuum International Publishing Group.

Furedi, F and Bristow, J (2008) *Licensed to hug: How child protection policies are poisoning the relationship between the generations and damaging the voluntary sector.* London: Civitas.

Giddens, A (1998) *The third way: The renewal of social democracy.* Oxford: Polity Press.

Gilligan, R (2001) *Promoting resilience: A resource guide on working with children in the care system,* London: BAAF.

Glasby, J and Littlechild, R (2009) *Direct payments and personal budgets: Putting personalisation into practice.* 2nd edition. Bristol: Policy Press.

Graham, M (2002) *Social work and African-centred worldviews.* London: Venture Press.

Graham, M (2007) Giving voice to black children: An analysis of social agency. *British Journal of Social Work*, 37 (8), 1305–17.

Goldberg, D and Huxley, P (1992) *Common mental disorders: A biosocial model.* Hove: Routledge.

GSCC (2004) *Codes of practice for social care workers.* London: GSCC. www.gscc.org.uk/

Haines, K and Case, S (2005) Promoting prevention: Targeting family-based risk and protective factors for drug use and youth offending in Swansea. *British Journal of Social Work*, 35 (2), 169–87.

Haringey Council (2008) *Haringey local safeguarding children board serious case review 'child A'.* www.haringeylscb.org/

Hargie, O and Dickson, D (2004) *Skilled interpersonal communication: Research, theory and practice.* Hove: Routledge.

Hatfield, B (2008) Powers to detain under mental health legislation in England and the role of the approved social worker: An analysis of patterns and trends under the 1983 mental health act in six local authorities. *British Journal of Social Work*, 38 (8), 1553–71.

Higham, P (2006) *Social work: Introducing professional practice.* London: Sage Publications.

Holland, S (2004) *Child and family assessment in social work practice.* London: Sage.

Hormans, G (1958) Social behavior as exchange. *American Journal of Sociology*, 62, 597–606.

Horwath, J (2001) *The child's world: Assessing children in need.* London: Jessica Kingsley Publishers.

Horwath, J (2007) The missing assessment domain: Personal, professional and organizational factors influencing professional judgements when identifying and referring child neglect. *British Journal of Social Work*, 37 (8), 1285–1303.

Howe, D (1995) *Attachment theory for social work practice.* London: Macmillan Press.

Howe, D (2009) *A brief introduction to social work theory.* London: Palgrave Macmillan.

Hunter, S and Ritchie, P (2007) *Co-production and personalisation in social care: Changing relationships in the provision of social care.* London: Jessica Kingsley Publishers (Research highlights in social work series).

International Federation of Social Workers and the International Association of Schools of Social Work (2001) *Ethics in social work, statement of principles*. Berne: IFSW. www.ifsw.org/p38000324.html

Jones, S (2009) *Critical learning for social work students*. Exeter: Learning Matters.

Jürgens, R (2008) *Nothing about us without us – Greater, meaningful involvement of people who use illegal drugs: A public health, ethical, and human rights imperative, International edition*. Toronto: Canadian HIV/AIDS Legal Network, International HIV/AIDS Alliance, Open Society Institute.

Kemshall, H (2002) *Risk, social policy and welfare*. Buckingham: Open University Press.

Kemshall, H (2007) Risk assessment and management: An overview. In Lishman, J (ed) *Handbook for practice learning in social work and social care: Knowledge and theory*. London: Jessica Kingsley Publishers.

Kemshall, H (2008) Risk assessment and management. In Davies, M (ed) *The Blackwell companion to social work*. 3rd edition. Oxford: Blackwell Publishing.

Koprowska, J (2008) *Communication and interpersonal skills in social work*. 2nd edition. Exeter: Learning Matters.

Koprowska, J (2010) *Communication and interpersonal skills in social work*. 3rd edition. Exeter: Learning Matters.

Laird, S E (2008) *Anti-oppressive social work: A guide for developing cultural competence*. London: Sage Publications.

Laming, H (2003) *The Victoria Climbié inquiry report. Cm5730*. London: The Stationery Office. Crown copyright. www.publications.parliament.uk/

Laming, H (2009) *The protection of children in England: A progress report*. London: The Stationery Office. Crown copyright. http://publications.everychildmatters.gov.uk/

Lau, A (2004) Family therapy and ethnic minorities. In K N Dwidedi (ed) *Meeting the needs of ethnic minority children*. London: Jessica Kingsley.

Leece, J (2002) Extending direct payments to informal carers: Some issues for local authorities. *Practice*, 14 (2), 31–44.

Leininger, M and McFarland, M R (2002) *Transcultural nursing*. New York: McGraw-Hill.

Levin, E (2004) *Involving service users and carers in social work education*. SCIE Guide 4. www.scie.org.uk/publications/

Lishman, J (ed) (2007) *Handbook for practice learning in social work and social care: Knowledge and theory*. London: Jessica Kingsley Publishers.

Macdonald, G (2007) Cognitive behavioural social work. In Lishman, J (ed) *Handbook for practice learning in social work and social care*. London: Jessica Kingsley Publishers.

McAuliffe, D (2005) I'm still standing: Impacts and consequences of ethical dilemmas in direct practice. *Journal of Social Work Ethics and Values*, 2 (1), 1–11. www.socialworker.com/jswve/

Main, M and Solomon, J (1986) Discovery of an insecure-disorganised/disoriented attachment pattern. In Brazelton, T and Yogman, M (eds) *Affective development in infancy*. Norwood, NJ: Ablex.

Manktelow, R (2008) Mental health social work. In Davies, M, *The Blackwell companion to social work*. 3rd edition. Oxford: Blackwell Publishing.

Means, R, Richards, S and Smith R (2008) *Community care: Policy and practice*. 4th edition. London: Palgrave Macmillan.

Millar, M and Corby, B (2006) The framework for the assessment of children in need and their families – a basis for a 'therapeutic' encounter? *British Journal of Social Work*, 36 (6), 887–99.

Miller, L (2006) *Counselling skills for social work*. London: Sage Publications.

Milner, R and Bull, R (1999) *Investigative interviewing: psychology and practice*. Chichester: John Wiley and Sons.

Milner, J and O'Byrne, P (2009) *Assessment in social work*. 3rd edition. Basingstoke: Palgrave Macmillan.

Minhas, B, Kaur, N, Hanson, E and Wyncoll, K (2002) *Culturally competent care: A good practice guide for care management*. Maidstone: Kent County Council.

Moss, B (2008) *Communication skills for health and social care*. London: Sage.

Munro, E (1999) Common errors of reasoning in child protection work. *Child Abuse and Neglect*, 23 (8), 745–58.

NIMHE (2005) *NIMHE guiding statement on recovery*. London: Department of Health.

Office of National Statistics (2000) *Psychiatric morbidity among adults living in private households in Great Britain*. Newport: ONS.

Office of Public Sector Information (1990) *National Health Service and Community Care Act 1990*. London: OPSI. www.opsi.gov.uk/ACTS/

Office of Public Sector Information (2009) *The Community Care, Services for Carers and Children's Services (Direct Payments) (England) Regulations 2009 No. 18*. London: OPSI. www.opsi.gov.uk/

Paniagua, F A (2000) *Assessing and treating culturally diverse clients: A practical guide*. 2nd edition. Los Angeles: Sage Publications.

Parham, T A (2002) *Counseling persons of African descent: Raising the bar of practitioner competence*. Los Angeles: Sage Publications.

Parker, J (2007) The social work process: Assessment, planning, intervention and review, in Lymbery, M and Postle, K (eds) *Social work: A companion for learning*. London: Sage.

Parker, J and Bradley, G (2007) *Social work practice: Assessment, planning, intervention and review*. 2nd edition. Exeter: Learning Matters.

Parker, J and Bradley, G (2010) *Social work practice: Assessment, planning, intervention and review*. 3rd edition. Exeter: Learning Matters.

Parrott, L (2006) *Values and ethics in social work practice*. Exeter: Learning Matters.

Parrott, L (2010) *Values and ethics in social work practice*. 2nd edition. Exeter: Learning Matters.

Parsloe, P (ed) (1999) *Risk assessment in social care and social work*. London: Jessica Kingsley Publishers.

Parton, N and O'Byrne, P (2000) *Constructive social work: Towards a new practice*. Basingstoke: Palgrave.

Payne, M (2005) *Modern social work theory*. 3rd edition. Basingstoke: Palgrave Macmillan.

Phillips, J, Ray, M and Marshall, M (2006) *Social work with older people*. 4th edition. London: Palgrave Macmillan.

Pinard, G-F and Pagani, L (eds.) (2000) *Clinical assessment of dangerousness: Empirical contributions.* Cambridge: Cambridge University Press.

Pithouse, A, Hall, C, Peckover, S and White, S (2009) A tale of two CAFs: The impact of the electronic common assessment system. *British Journal of Social Work*, 39 (4), 599–612.

Prime Minister's Strategy Unit (2005) *Improving the life chances of disabled people.* London: Prime Minister's Strategy Unit.
www.cabinetoffice.gov.uk/strategy/work_areas/disability.aspx

Pritchard, J (2007) *Working with adult abuse: A training manual for people working with vulnerable adults.* Jessica Kingsley Publishers.

Quinney, A (2006) *Collaborative social work practice.* Exeter: Learning Matters.

Rabiee, P, Moran, N and Glendinning, C (2009) Individual budgets: Lessons from early users' experiences. *British Journal of Social Work*, 39 (5), 918–35.

Reid, W J and Shyne, A W (1969) *Brief and extended casework.* New York: Columbia University Press.

Repper, J and Perkins, R (2003) *Social inclusion and recovery: A model for mental health practice.* Oxford: Bailliere Tindall.

Riddell, S, Pearson, C, Jolly, D, Barnes, C, Priestley, M and Mercer, G (2005) The development of direct payments in the UK: Implications for social justice. *Social Policy and Society*, 4 (1), 75–85.

Rogers, C (1961) *On becoming a person: A therapist's view of psychotherapy.* London: Constable.

Rutter, M (1981) *Maternal deprivation reassessed.* 2nd edition. Harmondsworth: Penguin.

Schaffer, H R and Emerson, P E (1964) The development of social attachments in infancy. *Monographs of the society for research in child development*, 29 (3) Serial No. 94.

Schirato, T and Yell, S (2000) *Communication and cultural literacy: An introduction.* 2nd edition. St Leonards, NSW: Allen and Unwin.

Seden, J (1999) *Counselling skills in social work practice.* Maidenhead: Open University Press.

Seden, J (2005) *Counselling skills in social work practice.* 2nd edition. Maidenhead: Open University Press.

Seddon, D, Robinson, C, Tommis, Y, Woods, B and Russel, I (2007) In their own right: Translating the policy of care assessment into practice. *British Journal of Social Work*, 37 (8), 1335–52.

Sharkey, P (2002) *The essentials of community care: a guide for practitioners.* London: Palgrave.

Shaw, I, Bell, M, Sinclair, I, Sloper, P, Mitchell, W, Dyson, P, Clayden, J and Rafferty, J (2009) An exemplary scheme? An evaluation of the Integrated Children's System. *British Journal of Social Work*, 39 (4), 613–26.

Sheldon, B and Macdonald, G (2009) *A textbook of social work.* London: Routledge.

Shepherd, E (1986) Conversational core of policing. *Policing*, 2, 294–303.

Sheppard, M (2009) High thresholds and prevention in children's services: The impact of mothers' coping strategies on outcome of child and parenting problems – six month follow-up. *British Journal of Social Work*, 39 (1), 46–63.

Sheppard, M and Grohn, M (2003) *Prevention and coping in child and family care: Mothers in adversity coping with child care.* London: Jessica Kingsley Publishers.

Smale, G, Tuson, G, Behal, N and Marsh, P (1993) *Empowerment, assessment, care management and the skilled worker.* London: NISW.

Social Work Task Force (2009) *Building a safe, confident future.* London: DCSF. http://publications.dcsf.gov.uk/

Spratt, T (2009) Identifying families with multiple problems: Possible responses from child and family social work to current policy developments. *British Journal of Social Work*, 39 (3), 435–50.

Sutton, C (1999) *Helping families with troubled children.* Chichester: Wiley.

Taylor, B J and Donnelly, M (2006) Professional perspectives on decision making about the long-term care of older people. *British Journal of Social Work*, 36 (5), 807–26.

Taylor, B and Devine, T (1993) *Assessing needs and planning care in social work.* Farnham: Ashgate.

Thompson, N (2005) *Understanding social work.* Basingstoke: Palgrave Macmillan.

Topss UK Partnership (2002) *National Occupational Standards for Social Work.* London: Skills for Care.

Trevithick, P (2005) *Social work skills: A practice handbook.* 2nd edition. Maidenhead: Open University Press.

van Ijzendoorm, M H, Goldberg, S, Kroonenberg, P M and Frenkel, O J (1992) The relative effects of maternal and child problems on the quality of attachment: A meta-analysis of attachment clinical samples, *Child Development*, 63 (4), 840–58.

Walker, S and Beckett, C (2004) *Social work assessment and intervention.* Lyme Regis: Russell House Publishing.

Webb, S A (2006) *Social work in a risk society: Social and political perspectives.* Basingstoke: Palgrave Macmillan.

Whittington, C (2007) *Assessment in social work: A guide for learning and teaching.* London: SCIE Knowledge guide 18. www.scie.org.uk/publications/

Wilson, C and Powell, M (2001) *A guide to interviewing children: Essential skills for counsellors, social workers and police lawyers.* Abingdon: Routledge.

Wilson, K, Ruch, G, Lymbery, M and Cooper, A (2008) *Social work: An introduction to contemporary practice.* Harlow: Pearson.

Wing, J K, Curtis, R H and Beevor, A S (1996) *HoNOS: Health of the nation outcome scales: Report on research and development July 1993 – December 1995.* London: Royal College of Psychiatrists.

Woolcock, M (2001) The place of social capital in understanding social and economic outcomes, ISUMA *Canadian Journal of Policy Research*, 2 (10), 11–17.

Index

Added to the page reference 't' denotes a table.

Transforming Social Work Practice titles in the series

To order, please contact our distributor: BEBC Distribution, Albion Close, Parkstone, Poole, BH12 3LL. Telephone: 0845 230 9000, email: learningmatters@bebc.co.uk. You can also find more information on each of these titles and our other learning resources at www.learningmatters.co.uk